D0078861

Ａ

BRUNEI

SABAH

SARAWAK

KALIMANTAN

STRAITS OF MAKASSAR

Rantepao

SULAWESI

O

N

E

S   I   A

Ujung Pandang

Surabaya

Yogyakarta

BALI

LOMBOK

CULTURAL SITES OF MALAYSIA, SINGAPORE, AND INDONESIA

CULTURAL SITES OF MALAYSIA, SINGAPORE, AND INDONESIA

Jacques Dumarçay and
Michael Smithies

Kuala Lumpur
OXFORD UNIVERSITY PRESS
Oxford Singapore New York
1998

Oxford University Press

Oxford New York
Athens Auckland Bangkok Bombay
Calcutta Cape Town Dar es Salaam Delhi
Florence Hong Kong Istanbul Karachi
Madras Madrid Melbourne Mexico City
Nairobi Paris Shah Alam Singapore
Taipei Tokyo Toronto

and associated companies in
Berlin Ibadan

Oxford is a trade mark of Oxford University Press

Published in the United States
by Oxford University Press, New York

© Oxford University Press 1998
First published 1998

All rights reserved. No part of this publication may be reproduced,
stored in a retrieval system, or transmitted, in any form or by any means,
without the prior permission in writing of Oxford University Press.
Within Malaysia, exceptions are allowed in respect of any fair dealing for
the purpose of research or private study, or criticism or review, as
permitted under the Copyright Act currently in force. Enquiries
concerning reproduction outside these terms and in other countries
should be sent to Oxford University Press at the address below

British Library Cataloguing in Publication Data
Data available

Library of Congress Cataloging-in-Publication Data
Dumarçay, Jacques.
Cultural sites of Malaysia, Singapore, and Indonesia/
Jacques Dumarçay and by Michael Smithies.
    p.   cm.
Includes bibliographical references and index.
ISBN 983 56 0028 7
1. Malaysia—Antiquities.   2. Singapore—Antiquities.
3. Indonesia—Antiquities.   4. Monuments—Malaysia.   5. Monuments—
Singapore.   6. Monuments—Indonesia.   7. Malaysia—Civilization.
8. Singapore—Civilization.   9. Indonesia—Civilization.
I. Smithies, Michael, 1932–   . II. Title.
DS593.D86   1998
959—dc21
97–19878
CIP

Typeset by Indah Photosetting Centre Sdn. Bhd., Malaysia.
Printed by Kyodo Printing Co. (S) Pte. Ltd., Singapore
Published by Penerbit Fajar Bakti Sdn. Bhd. (008974-T),
under licence from Oxford University Press,
4 Jalan Pemaju U1/15, Seksyen U1, 40150 Shah Alam,
Selangor Darul Ehsan, Malaysia

Preface and Acknowledgements

THIS volume follows our *Cultural Sites of Burma, Thailand, and Cambodia* published by Oxford University Press in 1995, and inevitably concentrates on, by far, the largest country in the region, Indonesia, with its long cultural history and vast wealth of archaeological and architectural sites.

To those who may have wondered why Vietnam did not appear in the earlier volume and why the Philippines does not in this, the answer is quite simply that neither has roots in the Hindu–Buddhist cultural background which dominates in the other countries of the region. Leaving aside the question of the small number of Cham monuments in Vietnam, the palaces of Hué have already been dealt with in another volume, and to venture into Spanish colonial and religious architecture in Luzon, Cebu, and elsewhere would take us away from the spheres of our concern.

We owe thanks to a number of people who have helped in the production of these two volumes, most particularly to Dr Dawn F. Rooney who, for the earlier volume, provided a number of excellent slides. Our gratitude also goes to the forebearance of our publishers and our families.

St Rémy lès Chevreuse
Bue Yai
May 1997

JACQUES DUMARÇAY
MICHAEL SMITHIES

v

Contents

Colour Plates

Plates

Figures

1 Introduction

As indicated in our previous volume, *Cultural Sites of Burma, Thailand, and Cambodia*, the civilizations of South-East Asia owe much to those of India, and the point will not be repeated here.

Historians and archaeologists have established a chronology for South-East Asian cultures, based on very varied sources: epigraphy, the chronicles, architectural or decorative styles, and archaeological discoveries, and over time have succeeded in forming a coherent framework in which a statue found in a temple can be as easily integrated as a text or a fresco. However, these sources are all presented to scholars as works complete in themselves: the time taken for their conception, composition, construction, or even, sometimes, commercialization, is not taken into account in the chronology. The construction of a building as complex as that of Borobudur, for example, was spread over at least two generations. In consequence, over such a relatively extended period, not only did techniques change, but so did the significance attached to the structure. Lastly, and this is not the least important, economic conditions changed from the time the undertaking was started to its completion fifty years later.

Chinese ceramics frequently serve as a point of reference for dating archaeological sites where often no other sources are available. The dates they provide, though, cannot be more than approximations; even if our knowledge of Chinese kilns and their rhythm of production is satisfactory, there are many grey areas, such as the length of time a particular model was used, the moment when its marketing was decided upon, or why one particular form rather than another was used. All this implies a choice, a decision taken long before a ceramic appears on a South-East Asian site. On top of this is added the way in which a piece was used, which depends on the very nature of the site. This is particularly true at Muara Jambi (Sumatra), where early strata have thrown up a great number of Chinese ceramics from the tenth and eleventh centuries, whereas the strata contemporary with the temples, of the fourteenth and fifteenth centuries, are almost entirely devoid of ceramics. This does not, of course, signify that Chinese influence in the region diminished, but merely that the nature of the site changed; it became a religious ensemble of shrines and stupa, where there were few occasions to break imported Chinese ceramics.

This is also true of the use of architectural treatises, in the sense that as one distances oneself from their place of origin, the date they are used loses all meaning. As an extreme example, one can take the work of the Italian architect Sebastiano Serlio (1475–1554), who wrote a book *Opere d'Architettura*, published in 1551. At the time it appeared, this treatise had considerable success and extensive influence, not only in Italy but also in France, but it was very quickly forgotten and replaced by the treatise of Palladio, which appeared in 1570. Rarely can the use of a treatise be so firmly dated. Yet it was only in the nineteenth century that the Javanese became familiar with these treatises and they used Serlio in particular for the Tuscan orders (the proportions indicated by Serlio, for this particular classical order, are quite special). This can be seen in several mosques in Jakarta, but at more or less the same time in Yogyakarta, the English translation, by Isaac Ware, of Palladio's treatise, was being used. In this example the chronological gap between the date of the treatise and its use is such that no one thought of dating the Langgar Tinggi Mosque in Jakarta to the sixteenth century, nor of placing Serlio and Palladio on the same basis. However, when, for example, one compares Balinese structures to their treatises, one needs to bear in mind the chronological gap between the writing and the realization, and also the fact that these treatises had been re-written many times (in the most recent Balinese version there is reference to ways of using reinforced concrete), which can only bring considerable incertitude to every attempt at chronological concordance between a structure and the text which inspired it.

The sites, certainly more than particular structures, involved a very long formulation. The choice of site, the hydrological conditions allowing sufficient water to be brought to it, and the establishment of a valid defence system around it, were difficult processes which not only involved technical knowledge but also required frequent invocations to the gods to ascertain if they favoured the enterprise.

The chronology of this process is well known for the site of Plered in Java. The decision to choose a new site for the residence of the ruler had to be taken immediately after the fire of Kerta in 1634. However, in spite of the devastation caused by the fire, construction work was only begun in 1644, at Plered. There were ten years of planning and doubtless hesitation. The choice was difficult: the site could not be too far from Kerta in order not to realign the centre of the kingdom, nor too far from a water source, and its defence had to be possible. Once the works started, they were rapidly brought to a conclusion; in 1647, the ramparts, moats, and the palace were sufficiently advanced for the court to remove to the new site. Meanwhile, the initiator of these works, Sultan Agung, had died, in 1646, and it was his successor, Amangkurat I, who profited by the new capital, which he continued to embellish and to try to protect from the possibility of flooding, at least until 1652.

The glory of Plered was particularly ephemeral. In 1660, the dam at Joho gave way and most of the area around the town was flooded.

2

Works were undertaken to regulate irrigation around the city and new buildings were constructed inside the ramparts until 1663, but it is likely that the decision to abandon Plered had already been taken in 1660, as a place exposed to flooding, though the move was not implemented until 1680, in favour of Kartasura. So, almost a generation passed between the desire to leave Plered and the installation of the court at a new site, by which time the historical context had changed in consequence of the war against Trunajaya, and even religious feelings were different.

Thus the time gap between the conception of a project and its realization can be seen to be significant. The choice of the site of Plered, beside the Opak River, was found to be disastrous, and it was probably fear of repeating the risks involved in Plered which led to the selection of Kartasura, which is far from any important water source. In the eighteenth century, when it was felt necessary once more to change the location of the court, the disaster of Plered had not been completely forgotten, and when Surakarta was selected, on the banks of the Solo River, considerable opposition was shown to the site, which was none the less retained, thanks to what was held to be divine intervention.

Thus, the dating of sites in insular and peninsular South-East Asia poses similar problems to those of the mainland, and caution has to be employed when using the evidence of ceramics, inscriptions, the chronicles, and architectural treatises.

2 Peninsular Malaysia and Singapore

Kedah

THE earliest archaeological sites discovered in Malaysia are those near the north-west coast in south Kedah. These have been extensively investigated, first by Quaritch Wales before the Second World War, and more recently by Alastair Lamb and Michel Jacq-Hergoualc'h. Wales, writing of the most substantial temple remaining, Candi Bukit Batu Pahat (Plates 1 and 2), remarked that the most notable feature 'as indeed of all Kedah temples, is the extreme lack of ornament, beyond a few plain mouldings' and pointed to a Kedah–Pattani land route for the transport of goods between the two sides of the peninsula.

1. Candi Bukit Batu Pahat, north face. (Jacques Dumarçay)

The vast site at Kedah, on the west coast of the Malay peninsula, in the basin of the Sungai Merbok and its tributaries, was occupied for a very long time, from the fifth to the fourteenth centuries, though its greatest period of prosperity lasted from the end of the twelfth to the thirteenth centuries. Two types of remains have come down to us: entrepôt zones and architectural elements (Fig. 1). The commercial sites have produced numerous ceramic shards, including pieces from the Chinese kilns of the Tang, Song, and Yuan dynasties, the Indianized states of mainland South-East Asia, and some fragments of Middle Eastern origin which is also the source of glass beads. These particular glass finds single out the originality of the site (there are others; in the peninsular part of Thailand, fragments of glass and beads have been found, and at Takua Pa, on the west coast, a Tamil inscription of the eighth century has been discovered).

The monuments constitute two types, Buddhist stupas and Hindu (usually Shivaite) temples. Attempts to reconstitute these have been undertaken several times. The remains of these buildings are extremely simple: a square *cella* raised on a simply compacted base, on which are found the supports for pillars which were either vertical or slightly inclined (Fig. 2; Plate 3). These techniques of construction derive for the most part from India where similar structures survive, particularly in Kerala, where there are numerous

2. Candi Bukit Batu Pahat, south face. (Jacques Dumarçay)

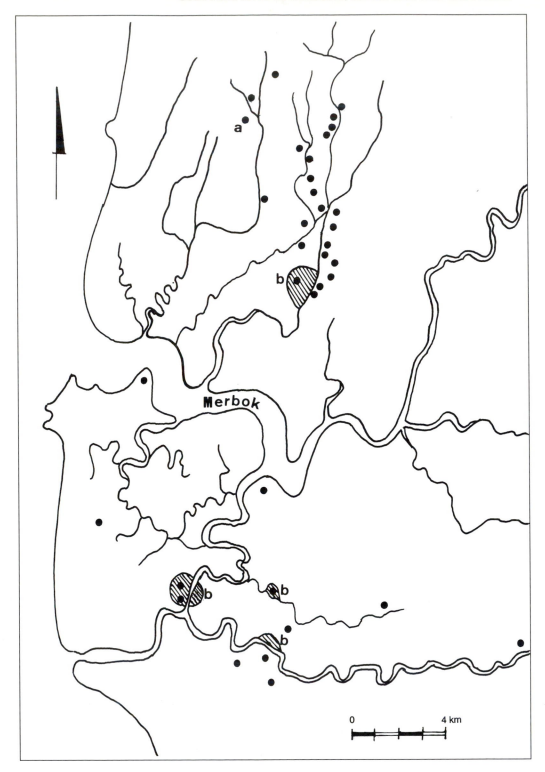

Fig. 1
Plan of archaeological sites in Kedah.

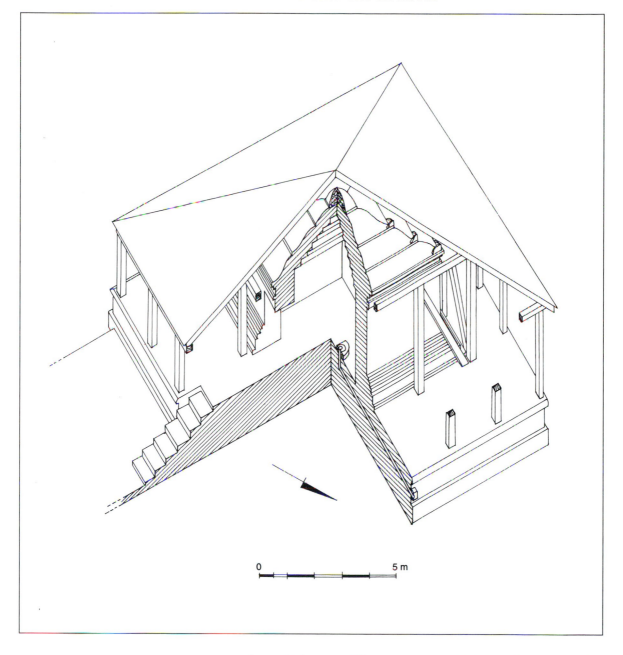

0 _____ 5 m

Fig. 2
Candi Bukit Batu Pahat (at 'a' in
Fig. 1), an attempted reconstruction of
the original superstructure.

temples entirely covered by a structure which functions as the sky,
and sometimes the nine planets are depicted on the ceiling. It can be
assumed, from the line of internal pillars, that the temples in Kedah
were of the same type. Similar temples exist in Cambodia and Java.

Opinion is divided as to whether these temples served the immig-
rant trading population or the indigenous Malays, none of whom
were converted to Islam at the time, as Ibn Batuta's account of his
journey of 1345–6 makes clear. What emerges from these excavations is that northern Malaya formed an important transit point

3. Laterite temple base, Kedah.
   (Jacques Dumarçay)

between the two sides of the peninsula, presumably indicating that the Singapore passage, famous for its ruthless and numerous pirates, was considered too dangerous by many traders involved in commerce between India and China.

Pulau Tioman

Nevertheless, many did still use the straits. There are numerous vestiges of the entrepôt trade passing through the Strait of Malacca and making use of Pulau Tioman, off the east coast of the Malay peninsula. There have been several archaeological excavations carried out on the island which show it was used as a stopping-off point from the eleventh to the twentieth centuries. The evidence on Tioman consists entirely of ceramic shards, mostly of Chinese origin, but including, from the fifteenth century, Thai and Vietnamese pieces, and, from the end of the nineteenth century to the early part of the twentieth, European wares (the most recent dates from 1920). Tioman was a provisioning point rather than a trading centre, and probably cargoes were rearranged here for more precise destinations than those given on departure.

Even when Tioman was not used to take on water, provisions, or trade goods, it still served as a geographical point of importance on the route between the Singapore Strait and both Siam and Vietnam (and beyond to China and Japan). Chaumont, the French ambassador to Siam in 1685, described 'Polimon' when he passed it, without stopping though, as 'a plentifull countrey' to which 'the Queen of Achem [Aceh] has some pretentions', sending some vessels there every year. Ceramic finds similar to those at Tioman have also been found at Kota Cina, near Medan in Sumatra.

Malacca

The major cultural site in Malaysia is undoubtedly Malacca. This city was the first established by Malays, possibly coming originally from Palembang in Sumatra, and bears numerous traces of its Portuguese, Dutch, and British occupations, though curiously the overall impression is of a dominant Chinese presence.

The founder of Malacca, Paramesvara (Iskandar Shah), is a person whose origins are disputed. The general consensus is that he was a prince of Palembang who ruled for three years (c.1388–90) before being ousted from Sumatra, possibly in a conflict with the Majapahit. He then appears to have spent some six years in Singapura (as Singapore was known until 1613), where he disposed of the local ruler, was ousted by the Siamese overlords of Singapura or their vassals, and spent a year moving from Singapura via Muar to Malacca. He founded this city either in 1399 or 1400, and reigned there until he died in 1413 or 1414. He was probably Mahayanist Buddhist, practising a form of Buddhism mixed with tantric and Hindu beliefs. Recent research indicates he never converted to Islam; this apostasy was performed by his grandson.

Paramesvara's new city initially led a somewhat precarious existence, surrounded by hostile kinglets, an expanding Javanese trade, and the reduction of private Chinese trade under the early Ming. The Chinese envoy Yin Ch'ing observed that Malacca was 'a prosperous chiefdom nominally subject to Siam' centring round an easily defensible hill. Paramesvara encouraged a Chinese presence in the city: the Chinese eunuch Admiral Zenghe (Cheng Ho, or Sam Po) paid several visits to Malacca; in 1409 he publicly declared Paramesvara king. Paramesvara, when an old man, accompanied by his wife and son, with a retinue of 570 persons, paid a visit to Peking, most probably in 1411, to acknowledge his submission. Being suzerain to China made Paramesvara, and the son who succeeded him, less vulnerable to possible Siamese attacks.

Things changed for Malacca in 1436; the third ruler returned from a prolonged visit to China, married a princess from Pasai, and converted to Islam. The most likely explanation for the conversion, which naturally the *Sejarah Melayu*, the 'Malay Annals', declares miraculous, was a way of attracting Muslim merchants, including the Javanese, to Malacca and gaining powerful allies in the process. The Islamization of the Malaccan court was a slow process, however,

9

and the Srivijayan courtly traditions were maintained; marriage alliances were contracted to strengthen the ruler's position.

Two Siamese attacks came, none the less, in the reign of a successor, but both were beaten off by the ruler's commander, Tun Perak. By the 1460s, Malacca controlled most of the southern Malay peninsula as well as Jambi and Bintang, and was instrumental in the propagation of Islam throughout the archipelago. It had undisputed control of the highly lucrative spice trade. Ma Huan (1451) in the *Ying-Yai Sheng-Lau* [The Triumphant Visions of the Shores of the Oceans] described Malacca as a city where a

sizeable stream flows by the royal palace before entering the sea. Over this the King has built a bridge, on which he has constructed some twenty booths for the sale of all kinds of commodities. Both the King and his subjects revere the laws of Islam.... In their trade transactions [the people] use tin. The language, the books and the marriage ceremonies closely resemble those of *Chao-wa* (Java).... There are four gates in the city wall, each furnished with watch- and drum-towers. At night men with hand-bells patrol. Inside the walls a second small enclosure of palisades has been built where godowns have been constructed for the storage of specie and provisions.

The reign of Mansur Shah (1456–77) saw Malacca at the height of its power. The bridge over the river was of stone, it was a cosmopolitan port, and according to Tomé Pires (whose *Suma Oriental* was written early in the sixteenth century and contains a wealth of information about early Malacca), forty-eight languages could be heard in the streets. The hinterland was little developed though, and apart from trade, the only occupation of the natives was fishing.

The appearance of the Portuguese in the region in 1509 was to affect the position of Malacca profoundly. Goa was captured in 1510, and Portuguese attentions soon turned to prosperous Malacca. The viceroy Alfonso de Albuquerque learnt of the wealth of the city, and the first Portuguese attack took place, to the amazement of the population which had no knowledge, so the *Sejarah Melayu* claims, of cannon balls and matchlocks. This attack was successfully beaten off, but the Portuguese soon returned. The second attack took place on 25 July 1511 and the final assault on 10 August; the bridge over the Malacca River was taken, the great mosque was invaded, and the sultan fled. In December 1511, Albuquerque loaded his spoils from the looted city on his flagship, the *Flor de la Mar*, which ran into a storm off Aceh, struck a reef, and sank.

The Portuguese at first were on the defensive, and built a stone fort, known as A Famosa, to safeguard the city; its most prominent feature was a watch tower some 36 metres high (the stone was obtained from Malay graves and buildings, and laterite blocks and bricks were used for the bastions and walls). By 1586, Malacca was a walled town and A Famosa a citadel within it (Plate 4). These defences were necessary; the Portuguese were surrounded by hostile Muslim forces, and between 1570 and 1575 had to withstand no less than three Achinese attacks on the city. In spite of all this

10

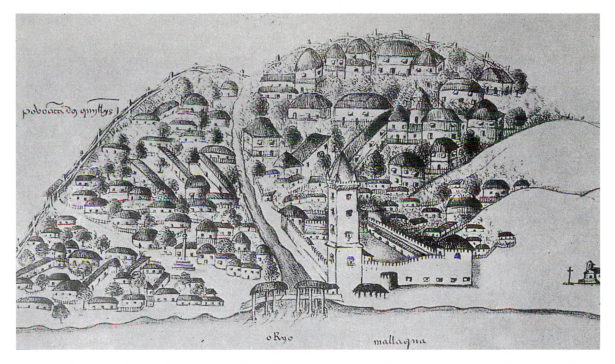

4. Sketch of Portuguese Malacca, from Gaspor Correia's *Lendas da India*, *c.*1540. (Instituto Cultural de Macau)

hostility, Malacca under the Portuguese prospered vastly, and the spice trade brought immense profits. The Indian community expanded at the expense of the Malays, and the Portuguese contracted many mixed marriages.

As Portuguese power in the region waned, its establishments in South-East Asia were increasingly coveted by the rising European power in the region, the Dutch. Malacca was attacked by Matalieff in 1606, and van der Haghen in 1615; it was permanently blockaded by the Dutch from 1633, and in 1640 they laid siege to the city, with some help from the Sultan of Johor (a descendant of the last Malay ruler of Malacca). The city offered strong resistance, but in January 1641, the ruined city was stormed by the besieging forces, and fell.

Malacca lost its importance with the departure of most of the Portuguese, though some continued to live there under the Dutch. Many moved to Batavia, which became the centre of the rice and spice trade; others moved to Portuguese outposts in Ceylon. The Indian population, which had collaborated with the Portuguese, also left. Justus Schouten came from Batavia to assess the considerable damage; among his recommendations was that the Portuguese church, Nossa Senhora de Annunciada, on top of the hill should be repaired, and made a temple of the Dutch Reformed Church. The Catholic Church was for a time banned, and only in 1702 was religious freedom proclaimed. Schouten was optimistic of Malacca's future, though his expectations were not fulfilled. Malacca survived as an unimportant Dutch outpost. The senior VOC (Dutch East India Company) employees had an easy life, plenty of slaves, and

11

country houses outside the town, just as in Batavia. The fort, flattened by the Dutch in their assault on the city, was reconstructed, and managed to withstand a Bugis attack in 1756.

Malacca was occupied by the British in 1795 as a consequence of the French invasion of Holland; the occupation was not opposed, and Dutch administrators continued to work there, though the Dutch governor and troops departed. Malacca's population was then only 1,500. The fort of A Famosa was demolished, and only the fortuitous passage of Raffles on holiday in 1808 stopped the destruction of the Santiago Gate, as a result of a report he wrote to Lord Minto, the Governor-General of India.

The city was handed back to the Dutch in 1818 as a consequence of the post-Napoleonic European settlement, but by the Anglo-Dutch Treaty of 1824, reverted to the British in exchange for the useless outpost of Bencoolen in Sumatra. Along with Penang and Singapore, it formed part of the Straits Settlements until the Second World War, and was absorbed into Malaya, later Malaysia, as one of the constituent states of the federation and, like Penang, without a hereditary ruler.

Nothing remains of the Malacca of Paramesvara, whose buildings were most likely to have been made of perishable materials, which offer little resistance to the tropical climate and less to the numerous attacks the city withstood over time. All that remains of Portuguese Malacca is the Santiago Gate at the base of the old fort of A Famosa. This bears a seventeenth-century date, which is when the fortress was restored by the Dutch, who placed their coat of arms above the entrance. Abdullah bin Kadir (1797–1854), who, as a boy, studied in the old fort at Malacca, has left a detailed description of the structure in his *Hikayat Abdullah*:

The bulwarks of the Fort sloped slightly inwards, with an ornamental stone projection running round its four sides. There were eight bastions varying in width from six to eight feet, which served as emplacements for artillery. The walls all round were about fifteen feet thick. Below each bastion there were underground living quarters fully provisioned, with wells and stables for horses.... The height to the top of the Fort was about sixty feet.... The Fort had four gates, one a big one in line with the large bridge and having in it a small door through which people went in and out after eight o'clock at night.... There were three bridges [so] constructed that they could be pulled up and down, and they used to be raised at night-time and during periods of riots or hostilities.... Inside the Malacca Fort there was a rise of moderate elevation, at the summit of which was the Dutch church.

The fort was destroyed by the British as they feared (quite unnecessarily as it turned out) a resurgence of Malacca; Crawfurd called this 'a piece of policy, equally barbarous and unnecessary'. Farquhar, then Resident, had some trouble in obeying his orders from Penang for its destruction, since the hundreds of coolies employed were terrified of the ghosts in the citadel, and all claimed to be laid sick by them; in the end he resorted to blowing it up with gunpowder. Abdullah bin Kadir again has many eye-witness details:

12

the Fort was the pride of Malacca and after its destruction the place lost its glory, like a woman bereaved of her husband, the lustre gone from her face.... The stonework of the destroyed Fort was carried away by people to all parts; some to build houses in Malacca, some to Batavia when the Dutch reoccupied Malacca recently, and some to Riau. The English too loaded pieces into ships to make warning buoys....

The ruined church, now dedicated to St Paul (Plate 5), on top of the hill which formed the centre of the fort, was built by the Portuguese in 1521. St Francis Xavier preached there, and for a time after his death, his body was interred there before being taken to Goa. A Portuguese bishopric was established there in 1577, with a diocese covering the whole of the Far East. The structure appears to have fallen into disrepair after the Dutch built their church at the foot of the hill. Crawfurd in 1828 wrote:

The Dutch, after getting possession of Malacca, used it as a Protestant church and burying-ground; and hence the unusual spectacle which it presents of the tombs of conquerors and conquered, Catholics and heretics, blended together in one spot. Without reading the inscriptions, the tombstones of the respective people are recognised by their age, and the different materials of which they consist. The Portuguese tombs are of granite from China, and the Dutch of a hard black trap rock from the Coromandel coast, for neither Malacca nor its vicinity afford either. Among the tombstones we read, in very distinct characters, and in the Latin language, the inscription on that of Dominus Peterus, second Bishop of Japan, who is

5. The ruins of St Paul's Church in the early 1830s. (From P. J. Begbie, *The Malayan Peninsula*, Madras: Vepery Mission Press, 1834)

said to have died in the Straits of Singapore in the year 1598. The body of St. Francis Xavier, the Apostle of the Indies, who died in China, once reposed here, but the sacred relic was disinterred and finally conveyed to Goa.

The Protestant Dutch built their own Christ Church in 1753, which retains its massive 13-metre wooden beams and old pews, though its porch was added in the nineteenth century. It is said that its bricks were shipped out from Holland and were faced with local laterite; certainly brick-making, like tile-making, became a Dutch monopoly in the late seventeenth century. It boasts many tomb-stones in its floor, but these are more recent than those to be found around St Paul's on the hill. The descendants of the Portuguese, whose original church fell into ruin, built in 1710 another church, St Peter's, slightly out of the old centre on what is now Jalan Bendahara; unlike its baroque counterparts in Goa, it is extremely simple, and reflects the relative poverty of the small surviving Portuguese community, which Crawfurd found to be 'all of the lowest order'.

The town square at the base of the hill on which the fort was found is now dominated both by Christ Church and the much older pink Stadhuys, or town hall, built by the Dutch around 1650 (Plate 6). This housed the VOC offices, and has solid brick walls,

6. Stadhuys and Christ Church, Malacca, from Auguste-Nicholas Valliant, *Voyage Autour du Monde Executé Pendant les Années 1836–7 sur la Corvette La Bonite*, Paris, 1852. (Muzium Negara, Kuala Lumpur)

14

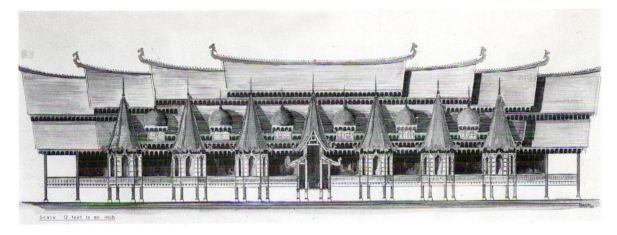

Scale 12 feet to an inch

7. An artist's impression of Sultan Mansur Shah's palace, *c*.1455. (Muzium Negara, Kuala Lumpur)

massive doors, and shutters on the outside, as well as fine wooden ceilings within. The brilliant salmon colour was apparently an innovation of the British in the early twentieth century, giving to the plaster coating on the walls the appearance of bricks. Prosaic remnants of the British period are found in the square outside, with a clock tower and a fountain dedicated to Queen Victoria. The only other substantial addition in the British period was a somewhat grand rest house, which has now been pulled down.

Not far from the Santiago Gate is the Melaka sultanate palace and museum, a wooden replica based on the description of Sultan Mansur Shah's palace (Plate 7) in the *Sejarah Melayu*:

The palace had seventeen bays, each interspace between the pillars being eighteen feet with pillars in circumference the span of a man's arms; the roof had seven tiers (? with seven pinnacles). Between were cupolas, and every cupola was finished with a dormer-window, its roof at right angles and terminating in flying crockets, all of them carved. Between the spires was trellis-work with pendant and pyramidal decoration. All the spires were gilded and their tops were of red glass, so that in sunlight they gleamed like fire. All the walls had eaves and inset were large Chinese mirrors that flashed in the sun like lightning, dazzling the sight.

There is also a replica of this palace in the grounds of the National Museum in Kuala Lumpur.

The Malacca River was always the focal point of trade at the time of the city's greatness; its sluggish, shallow and muddy waters today belie its wealthy past. Two parallel streets across the river still retain, for some, their Dutch names of Heeren and Jonkers streets. That is all that is Dutch about them, for they mostly comprise traditional Chinese shop-houses, of the 'one door, two windows' pattern: some are remarkably well preserved and have very fine carving as well as half-shutters at the door. Many of the structures in these streets are now given over to selling antiques. Two of Malaysia's oldest mosques are found in the Chinese quarter, Kampong Huli (1728) and Kampong Kling (1748), with unusual pyramid roofs and minarets. The third parallel street, Jalan Tukang Emas, has one of the first

15

Indian temples built in Malaysia in modern times, dating from 1781; this street leads into Jalan Tokong, which has the oldest Chinese temple in Malaysia, Cheng Hoon Teng (Plate 8), built in 1646. The external and internal decoration is elaborate, and the central altar is dedicated to the goddess of mercy Kwan Yin. The temple is associated with the visits of Admiral Cheng Ho; it contains a stone inscription commemorating his visit to the cemetery, outside the old town, known as Bukit China (Chinese Hill). The founder of this temple, Lee Wei King, was the second Kapitan China or leader of the Chinese community under the Dutch. It should be mentioned that, whereas the Chinese community barely existed under the Portuguese, it thrived under the Dutch who admired, and to some extent depended upon, the Chinese work ethic.

Bukit China is reputed to have been given originally to the daughter of a Chinese emperor sent to marry Sultan Mansur Shah in the 1460s. It was bought in the seventeenth century for the Chinese community by Lee Wei King and the cemetery is somewhat neglected today. At the foot of the hill is the Sam Po Kong temple, dedicated to the deified Admiral Cheng Ho. The well next to Sam Po Kong is variously termed the well of Hang Li Poh or Hong Lim Poh (Perigi Rajah in Malay) after the Chinese princess. However, it may well predate her arrival, since it has strong associations with Cheng Ho, who is supposed to have drunk from the well. The date attributed to the well, 1409, accords more with Cheng Ho than with one of the wives of Mansur Shah.

8. Cheng Hoon Teng, Malacca; reputedly the oldest Chinese temple in Malaysia. (Picture Library)

The other modest remnant of Malacca's past is St John's Fort, built in the eighteenth century by the Dutch on a slight eminence south of the town. Between the two sites lies the Portuguese settlement (Kampong Portugis), where the very mixed-blood descendants of the Portuguese remain, some still speaking sixteenth-century Portuguese, sometimes known as Cristão.

Crawfurd left Malacca in 1822 with gloomy prognostications for its future. But Malacca's prosperity had been a thing of the past after the departure of the Portuguese; the outpost was a drain on the financial resources of the VOC and then the East India Company; agriculture was neglected, and it was not until the beginning of the present century that the planting of rubber trees in the hinterland provided a substantial economic resource. While Malacca does still give the impression, in its old town, of a place where the past weighs down on the present, the modern town continues to thrive, if perhaps modestly and in some apparent disorder, outside its ancient perimeter.

The East Coast

The East Coast of the Malay peninsula boasts several sites of interest with numerous traditional palaces built in the nineteenth century. The term 'palace' in Malay usage is perhaps misleading; the wooden structures are for the most part simply rather larger and more carefully

9. Istana Tengku Sri Akar, Kota Bharu, Kelantan. (Jacques Dumarçay)

10. Istana Tengku Long, Kuala Trengganu, Trengganu. (Jacques Dumarçay)

crafted than most traditional Malay houses. The oldest extant palace is probably the Istana Balai Besar in Kota Bharu, Kelantan, built in 1844. The same town also contains the Istana Tengku Sri Akar (1886) (Plate 9). Trengganu had several palaces, most of which were moved over time. The Istana Tengku Long (*c.*1880) (Plate 10) was reconstructed in a park near Kuala Trengganu.

Singapore

The records of ancient Singapore are fragmentary, inconclusive, and sometimes contradictory. Marco Polo writes of Chiamassie (perhaps a corruption of Temasek), 'a large city on the island of Malayur speaking a language of their own and with their own king'. The Javanese text *Negarakertagama* of 1365 definitely speaks of a settlement called Temasek on Singapore Island. Wang Ta-yuan's *Description of the Island Foreigners* (1349) had its dominant hill (Fort Canning) 'resembling a trunkated coil rising to a hollow summit and surrounded by interconnected terraces' and mentioned that the 'natives and Chinese dwell side by side'. Wang considered that 'everything the inhabitants possess is a product of their plundering of Chinese junks'. These ships hoped to get past Tan-ma-hsi (Temasek) without encountering the several hundred pirate ships lying in wait. Ibn Said in the thirteenth century mentions black-armed pirates in neighbouring islands.

18

Temasek at the end of the fourteenth century appears to have had a moment of glory mentioned in the *Sejarah Melayu*, a source which has to be treated with circumspection. The supposed Srivijaya ruler at Palembang, Sang Utama, later known as Paramesvara ('prince consort'), is said to have seen the shore of Temasek and wanted to explore it, when a storm blew up and landed his party on the estuary of the present Singapore River, where he met a strange animal which he took to be a lion; he named the settlement he founded, Singapura, or 'Lion City'. Under his successors, Singapura 'became a great city, to which foreigners resorted in great numbers so that the fame of the city and its greatness spread throughout the world'. Some historians consider the Malay tradition of a great trading city a fiction, as Singapura/Temasek was not on the main maritime trading route between India and China at the time, which went through the Strait of Sunda between Sumatra and Java, or overland across the Malay peninsula to avoid the danger of the pirates near Singapura.

Portuguese sources, scarcely more reliable than the *Sejarah Melayu* since they were compiled a century after the events they describe, indicate that Paramesvara, known to Malays as Iskandar Shah, in about 1390, revolted against Javanese suzerainty, was driven from Sumatra, and came to Singapura/Temasek, murdered his host, and was driven from the settlement, possibly by the Siamese, who appear to have attacked Singapura in about 1400.

In the late fourteenth century Singapura seems to have been a minor Siamese dependency; after the founding of Malacca in about 1400, Singapura became subject to Malacca. When the Portuguese took Malacca in 1511, its Malay admiral fled to Singapura, and the successor sultan to Malacca, the ruler of Johor, kept a port official at Singapura. The Portuguese burnt down old Johor in 1587 and reported torching an outpost at the mouth of the Singapura River in 1613. This was probably the end of ancient Singapura.

The modern city-state of Singapore has almost no traces of its pre-colonial past, and little enough of its early days after its founding by Raffles in 1819. The newly established settlement was, however, laid out in an orderly fashion, and the old centre, in spite of all the trans-formations of the last thirty years or so, still retains this plan (Plate 11) as well as many of the original street names.

Singapore Hill, with its flagstaff, was retained as an open area, with a botanical garden at its foot (the botanical garden was de-veloped on its present location beyond Tanglin in the 1860s). The hill was sometimes known as Flagstaff Hill, Bukit Larangan ('Forbidden Hill'), or Government Hill (the governor's residence was located here in the early years of the settlement), and achieved its present name, Fort Canning Hill, in 1860, when a newly con-structed fort on the site was named after Viscount Canning, then Governor-General of India.

The old South-East Asian hand and amateur archaeologist, John Crawfurd, who became Resident of Singapore in 1823, visited

19

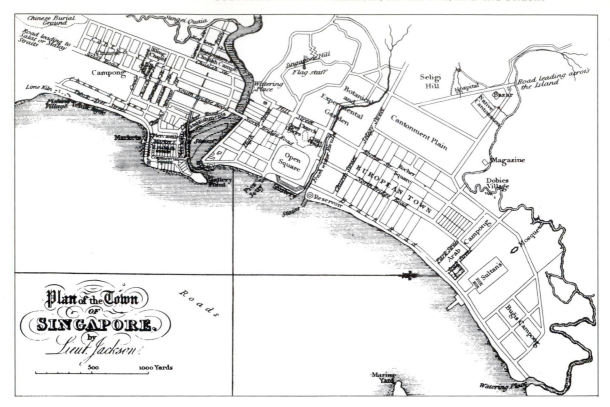

11. Plan of the town of Singapore, by Lieutenant Jackson, showing Singapore Hill. (From John Crawfurd, *Journal of an Embassy to the Courts of Siam and Cochin China*, 1828; reprinted Singapore: Oxford University Press, 1967)

Singapore in February 1822, on his way to Siam and Cochin-China as envoy of the East India Company, and left a detailed description of the remains of its ancient fortifications, concluding that they were not meant to withstand attack from the sea or the use of firearms. He also described a sandstone inscription discovered there, which, though nearly illegible in parts, he thought to be in Pali.

On the hill, he noted, were found numerous fragments of both Chinese and native pottery, as well as 'Chinese brass coins of the tenth and eleventh centuries'. Among the brick ruins of the hill was a terrace with 'fourteen large blocks of sand-stone; which, from the hole in each, had probably been the pedestals of as many wooden-posts which supported the building,' and in the centre was a circular enclosure, like a well, which he surmised may have formed the pit over which a Buddha statue would have been raised. There was another terrace with the supposed burial place of Iskandar Shah, which he put down as being apocryphal.

A cache of gold ornaments, probably Majapahit, was found in 1926 when excavations were made for a reservoir. Miksic conducted excavations in 1984 on Fort Canning Hill which was first described by Crawfurd. The shards discovered were late Song and early Ming (mid-thirteenth to late fourteenth century) and there are some blue-and-white fragments dating to around 1400. Miksic considers the place 'may have been either a sanctuary or a roofed hall with

20

wooden pillars and open sides, the *balai* of classical Indonesian architecture', such as can be seen on the recently exposed terraces at Kraton Ratu Boko near Prambanan in central Java.

The stone seen and described by Crawfurd in great detail was unfortunately blown up by government engineers in 1843 to provide space for quarters of the commander of Fort Fullerton. Thus went up in smoke the one epigraphic record of ancient Singapore. However, Colonel James Low managed to salvage three fragments of the stone and sent them to Calcutta, where they arrived in 1848. One fragment is now in the Singapore Museum; it has been dated to between 1230 and 1360. This was probably 'the rock which exists to this day in the moat of Singapura' which the *Sejarah Melayu* maintains was formerly the house of a treacherous treasury official of Iskandar Shah, turned 'by the will of Almighty God' into a stone.

3 Sumatra

THERE is little relationship between the number of known ancient sites on the coast of Sumatra and those inland on this huge island (Fig. 3). Because of its geographical situation astride major maritime routes and in spite of its size, the island is essentially oriented towards the sea, and its economy is based on commerce rather than agriculture.

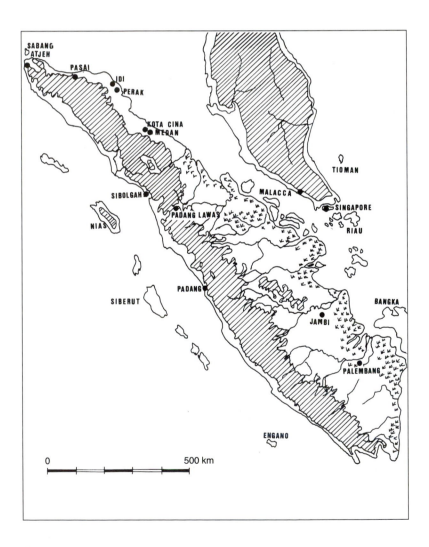

Fig. 3
Location of the principal cultural sites in Sumatra.

Aceh

The site of Aceh (Atjeh) is a good illustration of a city open to the sea, with a hinterland unfavourable to agricultural pursuits. One of the main concerns of the sultans of Aceh was always to ensure a sufficient supply of rice for the town.

It was probably during the fourteenth century that traders introduced from India the cultivation of pepper in the region, but it was only in the sixteenth century that Aceh began to assume some importance. The seizure of Goa and later Malacca, in 1511, by the Portuguese altered the trading patterns in pepper, causing the traders displaced by the Portuguese between the Malabar coast and Aden to provision themselves from more distant Sumatra.

The approach to Aceh was difficult (Fig. 4), the town being built on the banks of the Kali Aceh which splits the conurbation into two.

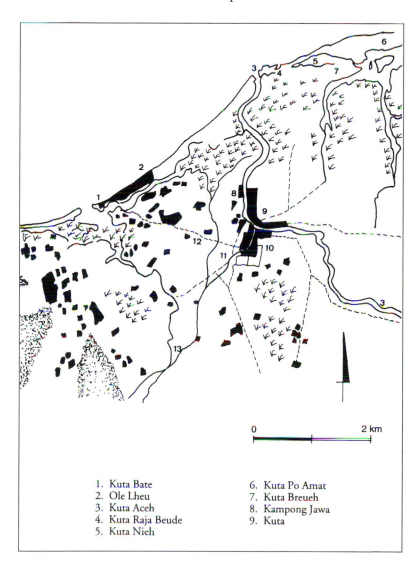

1. Kuta Bate
2. Ole Lheu
3. Kuta Aceh
4. Kuta Raja Beude
5. Kuta Nieh
6. Kuta Po Amat
7. Kuta Breueh
8. Kampong Jawa
9. Kuta

Fig. 4
The agglomeration of Kuta Raja in old Aceh.

It was only easily reached by going up this stream on barges from its mouth, as sea-going vessels were too large. The estuary is located deep inside a bay which is not easily entered as it is protected by a chain of formidable islets which often caused shipwrecks. These natural defences were complemented by a fort which overlooked the estuary.

It was during the reign of Sultan Iskandar Muda (1607–37) that Aceh achieved its period of greatest prosperity (his reign was the subject of a study by Denys Lombard, who is to be credited with the essential points of this brief survey). The resources of Aceh at this period comprised petrol extracted from the Deli region, sulphur, camphor, benzoin, and gold; to these largely traditional products were added, from the fourteenth century, silk and pepper. It was above all pepper which became the principal export of Aceh and formed the main source of the taxes collected on commodities, which filled the sultan's treasury. Ships paid to enter and leave the port, and customs dues were carefully supervised.

In spite of all the power which came with this extensive commerce, Iskandar Muda was not always victorious. The Achinese fleet scored some successes over the Portuguese based in Malacca, notably against Admiral Miranda in 1615, but in 1629, Iskandar suffered a serious reverse. The Portuguese tried to improve their relations in 1638 with Aceh after the death of the notoriously cruel Iskandar, but the Portuguese envoys were assassinated in unpropitious circumstances. The seizure of Malacca by the Dutch in 1641 was a serious loss to both the Portuguese and the Achinese, who never recovered. The centre of the pepper trade gradually shifted towards another state on the east coast of Sumatra, Deli, which freed itself from the suzerainty of Aceh in 1669. Nevertheless, at the beginning of the nineteenth century, Aceh was still an important pepper producer, though most of the trade passed through the pepper ports of Deli (Medan), Serdang, Batu Bara, and Asahan.

The influence of Aceh in the seventeenth century was due to the almost global trade which passed through it, and put it in contact with the Malay world, India, the Middle East, and Europe. Even if the economic tools of the Achinese appear uncouth (the term 'piracy' is often used), they were for the period relatively subtle: the use of devaluation reveals a concept of monetary manipulation which was exceptional in the region.

The site of Aceh assumed political importance again in the second half of the nineteenth century. Pepper production peaked at some 15 000 tonnes in 1820, but the world market could not absorb such a large quantity, with the result that prices dropped markedly. The Achinese Sultan Ala'ad-din Mansur Shah (1838–70) charged his son Husin with re-establishing Aceh's authority over the principalities of Langkat, Deli, and Serdang, putting a fleet of 200 vessels at his disposal. The sultan became a pepper rajah who could fix his prices, but the trade was almost entirely with the English, which the Dutch did not approve of.

24

The Dutch governor in the first instance sent a gunboat, the *Bromo*, off Aceh in December 1862, and wrote to the sultan, calling on him to send an envoy to Riau to determine the frontiers of the east coast states, which would have had the result of restricting Aceh's exports. This diplomatic manoeuvre was accompanied by military action, involving the entry of Dutch troops into the state of Asahan. The sultan sought assistance from the British in Penang, but help was not forthcoming. The very well-known Aceh War began with a first expedition in 1865, and the Dutch broke into the Aceh palace in 1873. The sultanate was officially annexed in 1874, but resistance continued sporadically until the end of the century.

Banda Aceh today is a bustling, noisy city with few souvenirs of its past. The principal mosque is an attractive building in the centre, the construction of which was started in 1879 by the Dutch. The Gunungan garden, said to have been built for the Malay wife of a sultan in the seventeenth century, is a combined playground and bathing place with imitation hills. Opposite it is a low gate giving access to the former palace.

The archaeology of the many ports on the north-east coast has not yet been closely studied, but information is available about their activities from travellers' accounts. At the end of the thirteenth century, when Marco Polo began his presumed return journey to Europe, he stayed five months in Pasai (Samudra) as well as in Perlac, which were both at the time important naval stations, in particular Pasai, which served as a base for the Chinese admiral Cheng Ho, who conducted seven missions in the region between 1403 and 1433. The remains of the entrepôts are found on the maritime route along the east coast of the Malay peninsula and passing through the Strait of Malacca. Tioman has already been mentioned in the chapter on Malaysia.

North Sumatra

Kota Cina
Kota Cina, near Medan, which was active from the twelfth to the fourteenth century, has been the subject of archaeological investigations.

The main trade in Kota Cina was in ceramics, but unlike Tioman it was not the only trade. Several black jasper touchstones have been discovered, indicating some trade in gold and silver. Contacts with India must have been numerous, and a small Shivaite temple was found on the site. The provenance of the ceramics covers a broader geographical area than Tioman up to the fifteenth century, and extends to Iran.

Medan itself is now the third largest city in Indonesia, though in 1823 it had only 200 inhabitants. Its prosperity grew with the establishment of tobacco as a plantation crop, and was made the capital of North Sumatra by the Dutch in 1886. The Sultan of Deli's palace was built in 1888, and the great mosque in 1906.

Lake Toba

The area around Lake Toba is the heartland of the Bataks, a distinctive people with a fearsome reputation in battle and for ritual cannibalism. Prapat is the starting-point for the visit to Samosir Island in the middle of the lake, which counts remarkable Batak houses with sagging ridge poles and huge gables, and a number of old carved stone sarcophagi among its many attractions. The area has seen considerable growth in tourism in recent years.

Padang Lawas

In the interior, the monuments at Padang Lawas are of the same period as those at Muara Jambi, that is, the fourteenth and fifteenth centuries, and one of the sites, Bahal, appears to have had a similar evolution. After having been a commercial entrepôt linked to the internal distribution of the island from the eleventh to the thirteenth

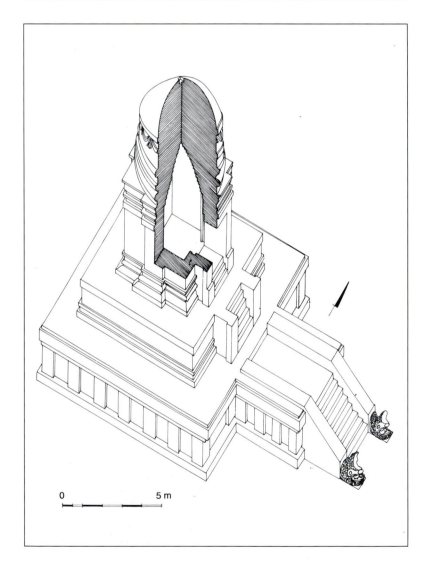

Fig. 5
Candi Bahal I at Padang Lawas.

0   5 m

centuries, it became, at the end of the fourteenth century, a religious site given over to a form of tantric Buddhism which gave rise to erotic sculpture. Bahal must have comprised a great number of buildings, but today only three are reasonably well preserved. Candi Bahal I (Fig. 5; Plate 12) is a brick construction with a slight inclination northwards of 10 degrees (the same orientation is found with the other two sanctuaries). The tower rises from a broad base decorated with reliefs showing dancers and musicians; the entrance doorway has been destroyed, apart from the two pilasters which framed it, decorated with two naked guardians. The temple is reached by a very narrow stairway. The upper part is in the form of a stupa, around the base of which is a broad garland. Bahal II has a similar plan and structure, while Bahal III again is similar, but with the

12. Candi Bahal I, Padang Lawas.
(Jacques Dumarçay)

upper part in the form of a tower, unfortunately in a very poor state of preservation. Near by, to the east of Bahal, at Pulo, can be seen the remains of a huge brick stupa which was topped by a cluster of stone parasols which are now lying on the ground.

Muara Jambi

Muara Jambi is situated on the left bank of the Jambi River (Plate 13), some 15 kilometres below the town of Jambi and approximately 72 kilometres from its estuary. Access is mainly by boat, since, except at the height of the dry season, the site constitutes an island with very marshy banks.

Several archaeological investigations have been carried out at this site, in particular at Candi Astana (1 in Fig. 6), and probes have been conducted at all the most obvious places. It appears there were at least two main periods, which can be subdivided into a number of different levels. In the first instance, from the tenth to the twelfth centuries, it seems likely that the island served as an entrepôt; there are numerous Chinese ceramic shards, and the forms and origins of these ceramics, coming from Guandong and Fujian, are very similar to those found not only at Kota Cina and Tioman (Malaysia), but

13. The river at Jambi. (Jacques Dumarçay)

also fragments discovered at Palembang and, in Java, at Banten. Variations in the trade of these ports came not from the imports but from the exports: pepper in the north of the island, precious metals at Kota Cina, rattan and rare wood from Jambi, tin from Palembang, and again pepper and precious metals from Banten.

At a later period, from the thirteenth to the end of the fifteenth century, the island of Muara Jambi was dotted with religious constructions; more than forty have been located to date. Commercial activity did not stop, but went upstream, probably to the site of the modern town of Jambi. The monuments have all been cleared of their forest cover and their meaning has been generally identified; they are mostly Buddhist structures some of which contained some very fine statues, as with the Prajnaparamita of the fourteenth century discovered in the excavations of Candi Gompong (3 in Fig. 6). The enclosure of this temple contained at each corner an iron *vajra* (the symbol of the lightning struck by Indra). A similar discovery was made at Candi Tinggi (2 in Fig. 6). These objects defined the space in which the temple was placed, and probably were left as an indication that the ritual of implantation had been carried out. The priest in charge struck the ground with one of the *vajra*, which transformed the earth by symbolically 'vitrifying' it, or sometimes

Fig. 6
Site plan of Muara Jambi showing main excavations.

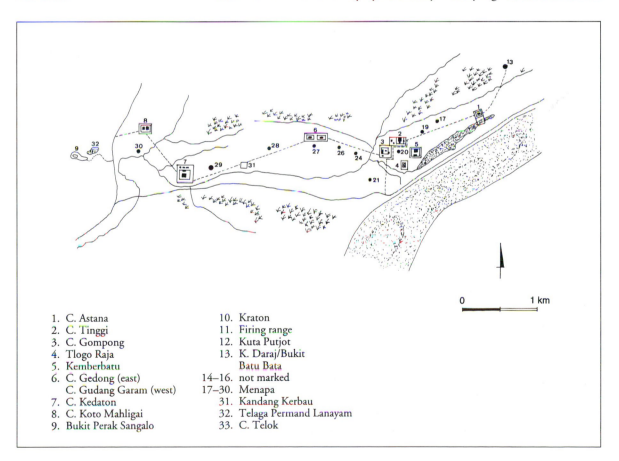

1. C. Astana
2. C. Tinggi
3. C. Gompong
4. Tlogo Raja
5. Kemberbatu
6. C. Gedong (east)
   C. Gudang Garam (west)
7. C. Kedaton
8. C. Koto Mahligai
9. Bukit Perak Sangalo
10. Kraton
11. Firing range
12. Kuta Putjot
13. K. Daraj/Bukit
    Batu Bata
14–16. not marked
17–30. Menapa
31. Kandang Kerbau
32. Telaga Permand Lanayam
33. C. Telok

transforming it into a diamond. On this now transmogrified surface, a mandala was traced (the design has been discovered at Candi Gompong). This outline determined the position of the small structures in which were placed a symbol or (in the case of Candi Gompong) a letter of the Sanskrit alphabet representing a god, and the whole constituted a theogony. At Candi Gompong it was most probably a Vajradathu mandala defining the relationship between the Vairocana Buddha and the Buddhist pantheon.

The monuments of Muara Jambi are all built of brick and their advanced decay only allows for the restoration of the base with a degree of certainty. Candi Astana (1 in Fig. 6) is in the form of a terrace which has undergone several changes and which was designed to be covered by a stupa in its first state, and then, later, an important seated statue. Candi Tinggi (2 in Fig. 6) was restored at the beginning of the 1980s, and comprises a very high base which originally was topped by an important stupa which today does not exist. In the courtyard of the monument are several small stupa. The surrounding wall is built using the technique of double facings, traditionally used in stone monuments, and which consisted of two outer walls containing a mixture of brick debris mixed with mud in between. Candi Gompong (3 in Fig. 6) also had a very high foundation of solid brick, with niches projecting from the axes; in one of these was found the statue mentioned above. The internal filling is not always brick; for example, Candi Kedaton (7 in Fig. 6; Fig. 7),

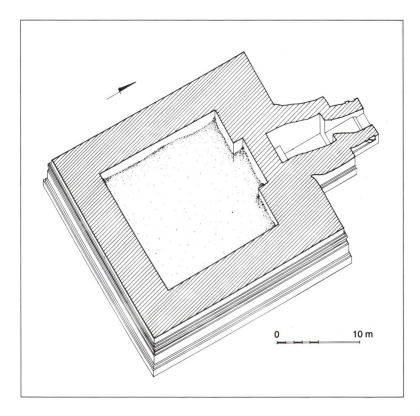

Fig. 7
Candi Kedaton at Muara Jambi.

30

now reduced to its foundation, had a brick wall more than 4 metres thick, and with a white stone infill. It is possible that this temple was not destined to be used by Buddhists, as most at the site were; its overall plan recalls that of Hindu temples in Java of the thirteenth or fourteenth centuries—a main shrine with three chapels facing it. On the same site is another structure, the Tlogo Raja (4 in Fig. 6), the purpose of which is uncertain; it comprises a rectangular pool surrounded by a water-filled canal enclosed by two dikes.

The small museum at Muara Jambi contains some of the objects discovered when the monuments were being cleaned and during the subsequent excavations, as well as very fine ceramics and bricks on which the construction workers had incised drawings of often considerable interest, in particular showing houses which allow for a summary restitution of the architectural environment of the temples (Fig. 8); the archaeological museum at Jambi also has some incised bricks. The buildings shown recall the huge Minangkabau houses in the Padang region in West Sumatra, with however one difference, which is probably due to the date of the drawings, the fifteenth century—they are closer to the prehistoric model which appears on the bronze drums of the South-East Asian region with, at the ridge, an indication of the stretcher which causes the roof to curve.

Fig. 8
Illustration of a structure on a carved brick from Candi Gudang Garam.

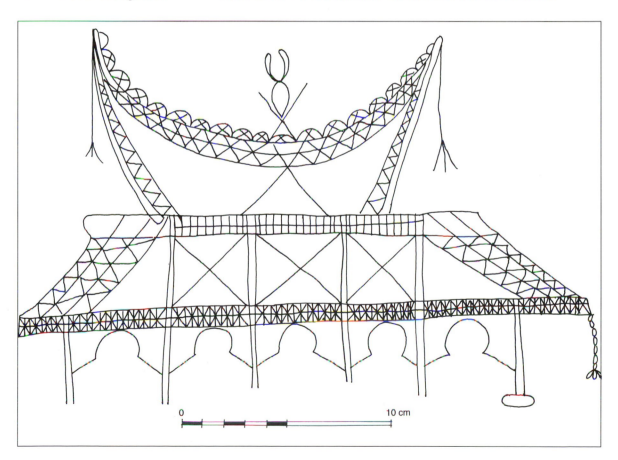

0   10 cm

Jambi has two museums worth seeing. An ethnographic collection is found in the very fine house dating from the end of the nineteenth century, and the archaeological museum has several remarkable pieces, including a monolithic stupa found at Selok Sipin in the region, and a bronze lamp imported from southern India in the twelfth or thirteenth centuries, at the time of the Chola dynasty, which demonstrates the continuity of links between Sumatra and the powerful rulers of southern India. In the eleventh century, a Srivijayan king ruling over the Jambi region ordered the construction of a temple at Negapatam, in Chola territory. However, the marked prosperity of the Jambi region probably occurred after the decline of Aceh, when the Jambi merchants cornered the market in all the pepper produced in the Minangkabau lands.

Palembang

The town of Palembang (Fig. 9) is located on the banks of the Musi, about 100 kilometres from its mouth in the Strait of Bangka. The region between Palembang and the coast is entirely covered by a thick mangrove forest through which ingress and egress is possible only along the numerous arms of the river.

When Ma Huan, the interpreter of Admiral Zenghe, stopped at Palembang in 1413–15, the region had been under the rule of the Javanese Majapahit dynasty since 1377, but the souvenir of the great kingdom of Srivijaya was still strong, and Ma Huan indicated Palembang was its capital.

The earliest mention of the kingdom of Srivijaya dates from 670, but the most important text for this period is that of the Chinese pilgrim I Ching, who undertook a vast journey in the last quarter of the seventh century. He admired, when he passed through Sumatra, the Buddhist monasteries he saw there, but his journey is particularly important for showing how extensive were the contacts between India and China through the Strait of Malacca.

The excavations recently conducted at Palembang prove, by the discovery of Tang dynasty Chinese ceramics, that trade with China existed from the eighth century. Apart from archaeological finds, there are few important remains of the Srivijaya period in Palembang. However, the excavations conducted by P. Y. Manguin on Bangka Island, at Kota Kapur, revealed a small Vishnuite temple of the seventh century, probably indicating that tin from Bangka was already being exploited.

All these discoveries justify without further doubt Ma Huan's identification of the capital of Srivijaya as Palembang. From the seventh century, the city was flourishing and imported precious items from China; numerous celadon shards have been found, and tin was most likely exchanged for ceramic pieces. Nothing remains of this prosperous city; it seems likely to have been similar to the modern town of Sungsang (Plate 14), located at the mouth of the Musi, and entirely built on piles. This is also the case with Upang,

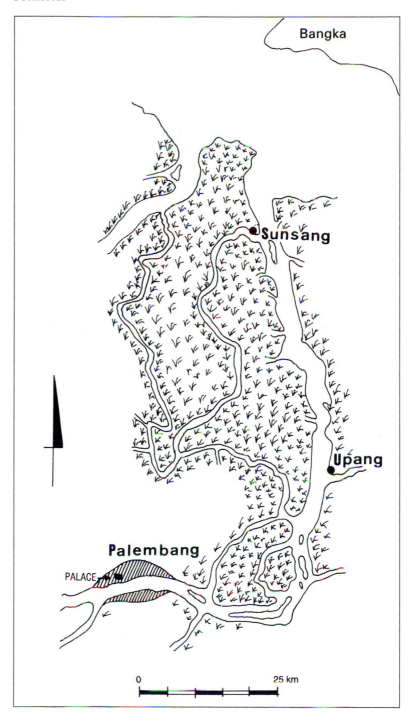

Fig. 9
Palembang, showing the location of the palace.

the name of which appears on one of the rare inscriptions linked with the kingdom of Srivijaya.

The earliest remains of any importance at Palembang probably date from the Javanese occupation of the fourteenth century. They

14. Sungsang, a village built over water at the mouth of the Musi leading to Palembang. (Jacques Dumarçay)

are located in the middle of the city, at Geding Suro, and comprise several buildings, the original function of which is uncertain. They constitute brick foundations for wooden structures. Building I was rectangular, with perpendicular projections, and a wall decorated with finials. Building II must have been altered many times, but the bases to secure the wooden posts of the superstructure remain and can be seen. The fact that during the Muslim period Geding Suro served as a cemetery makes further identification somewhat problematic (Plate 15).

After a particularly confused period, Islam was established in Palembang and a sultanate created. These sultans were great builders, not only in the town, but also outside it, where vast gardens were created with complex hydraulic installations. In 1737, a huge palace was built on the banks of the Musi, but was destroyed and replaced in 1834 by the present palace (Fig. 9), which was recently converted into an archaeological museum, the Badaruddin Museum (Plate 16). This contains a very interesting collection, in particular the huge prehistoric sculptures of Pasemah. There are also remains of a late eighteenth-century Dutch fort in the city.

34

15. Muslim tombs in Geding Suro, Palembang. (Jacques Dumarçay)

16. Nineteenth-century palace in Palembang, now converted into an archaeological museum. (Jacques Dumarçay)

West Coast Sites

The west coast of Sumatra has no known ancient settlements, but the pepper trade made it important in the colonial period. Benkulu (Bencoolen) was a British settlement from 1685, established after the Dutch conquest of Banten, but it was never successful and mortality was high. The British thankfully exchanged Bencoolen for the, by then, equally useless Malacca in 1824. Fort Marlborough is the remnant of the eighteenth-century colonial period.

Padang is the centre of the distinctive matriarchal Minangkabau people who nevertheless manage to reconcile their traditional beliefs with Islam (Plate 17). House forms are remarkable for their size and projecting multiple roof outlines (Plate 18). The new museum is built in this tradition and has an interesting collection of antiques. To the north of Padang lies Bukittinggi in the mountains, which has become a prime Minangkabau cultural centre; the museum is an excellent example of traditional house construction. Fort de Kock is a Dutch construction built to counter the fanatical Muslim Padri rebellion from 1821 to 1837, which attempted to overthrow traditional Minangkabau as well as Batak culture.

Off the west coast of Sumatra lies a parallel chain of islands, the most famous of which is Nias. This has three different architectural

17. Mosque in Padang, Sumatra.
(Jacques Dumarçay)

18. Minangkabau house near Padang.
(Jacques Dumarçay)

traditions of housebuilding, the most impressive being in the south of the island, with huge roofs resting on very complex beamwork. The animistic Nias islanders had a distinctive culture of their own, which included male initiation rites requiring leaping over piles of stones, local carving traditions, and stone tables on which the dead were laid out to decay.

In spite of its wealth, or rather because of it, and the frequent cupidity this gave rise to on the part of the Javanese, Chinese, Indians, Portuguese, and Dutch, Sumatra was not able to develop a cultural heritage comparable to that of Java. Further excavations and accidental discoveries may perhaps change this impression, but it seems unlikely that any great architectural ensemble will be found. Interest in the Sumatran heritage is different, and in it can be seen, above all, the contacts which commerce gave rise to, as virtually the whole world passed through the Strait of Malacca or the Sunda Strait, and stopped in Sumatra.

4 Java

THE island of Java is extremely rich in cultural sites but here only a summary indication will be given of them, proceeding from west to east. This archaeological abundance is not equally distributed throughout the island nor through all historial periods. From the eighth to the tenth centuries, the centre was the most dynamic; from the eleventh to the fourteenth centuries the eastern part was dominant, and then, from the fifteenth to the the eighteenth centuries, the north coast demonstrated considerable activity, which shifted during the eighteenth century to the centre of the island once more. In the west, the Sunda region was less productive, more austere, and politically less well organized. This is why it was relatively easy for the Dutch to begin their colonization process from here.

West Java

Banten

Banten (Bantam) is located on the north coast, at the western extremity of the island, close to the Strait of Sunda (Fig. 10); the site was first occupied very early in historic times. The excavations

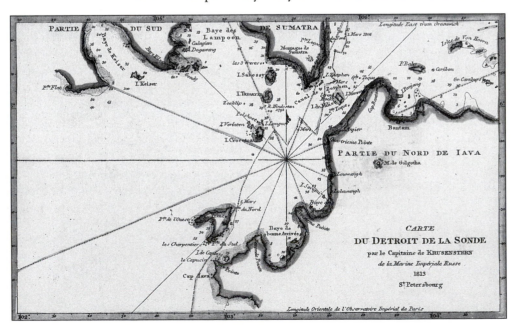

Fig. 10
Map of the Strait of Sunda, drawn by Captain de Krusenstern, St Petersburg, 1813.

directed by Claude Guillot have enabled its past to be more clearly established and his publications are the source of the essential points of this summary.

The discovery of an inscription near Monjul, similar to those found near Jakarta, demonstrates that the very ancient Vishnuite kingdom of Taruma, of the fifth to the seventh centuries, extended to the Sunda Strait. This kingdom was superseded in the region by the Srivijaya empire, established towards the end of the tenth century at a time when political weakness in central Java caused the power base there to shift progressively to the east. The suzerainty of Srivijaya appears to have been effective to the end of the twelfth century. In this period, the town of Banten was located 10 kilometres to the south of the present site, at Banten Girang (close to the modern town of Serang), away from the coast, on a small outcrop of volcanic tuff. The town was surrounded by a rampart with a double moat. Nothing remains of the structures inside this enclosure, but many ceramic and other objects have come to light. These Chinese ceramic imports are slightly different from those of the Sumatran ports; there appears to have been less variety in the types, and the quality is decidedly inferior. But the origin of the pieces found is similar to the sources of the Sumatran imports, namely the southern Chinese kilns. In addition to these ceramic imports, which included Thai and Vietnamese pieces, varied forms of local pottery were found, as well as fairly numerous iron tools and two stone adzes. It seems likely, given the position of this discovery, that these pieces, to all appearances of prehistoric origin, were still used at least until the thirteenth century. A small goldsmith's workshop, with a crucible and a lump of borax, the natural fondant of gold, were also found.

Banten Girang continued to prosper because of the pepper trade; the cultivation of pepper was introduced in the region in the twelfth century. However, in 1527 Muslim forces, assisted by the Sultan of Demak, took possession of Banten Girang, which was not completely abandoned, but the capital was transferred to the coast (Fig. 11). On this site there are numerous vestiges of the past. At the beginning of the sixteenth century the grand mosque was built; it was burnt down, destroyed, and reconstructed many times, but always with the same plan and the same height, in particular its five superimposed roofs which were already admired by travellers in the seventeenth century. The minaret was built in about 1620 and the Surosowan Palace at the end of the seventeenth century, both demonstrating the prosperity of the port of Banten (Plate 19).

But the ruler at this period, Sultan Ageng (r. 1651–82) tried to seize Cirebon, which worried the Dutch in Batavia who feared, with some justification, being encircled. A conflict between the two arose, and Banten lost forever its independence. The Dutch built their Fort Speelwick right on the coast.

Associated with Banten and 2 kilometres to its south is an artificial lake with an island, Tasikardi, in the middle, built in the seventeenth century, and transformed in the eighteenth century into

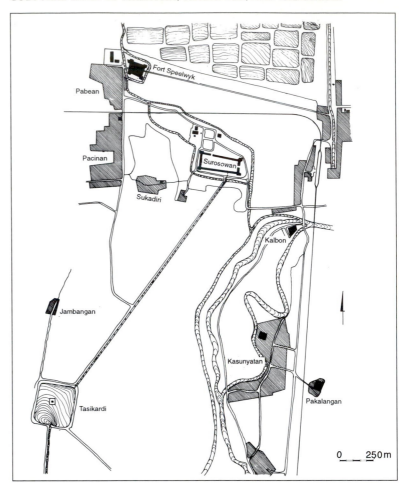

Fig. 11
General plan of Banten Lama.

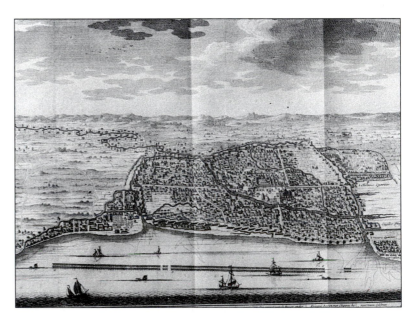

19. Port of Banten, from Francois
    Valentijn, *Beschryving van
    Groot Djava ofte Java major*,
    Amsterdam, 1726. (Jacques
    Dumarçay)

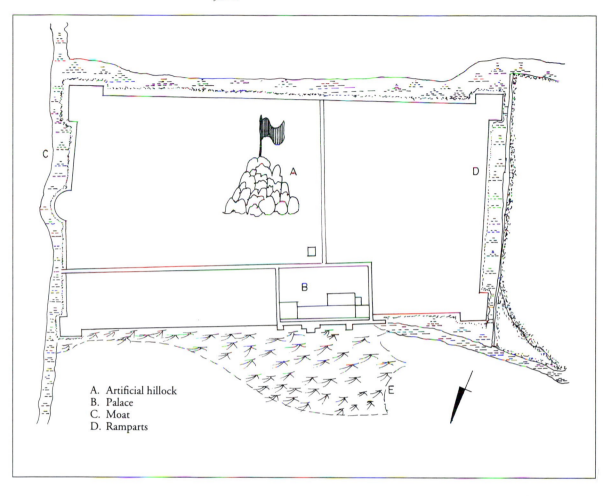

A. Artificial hillock
B. Palace
C. Moat
D. Ramparts

Fig. 12
Plan of the fortifications of Tirtayasa, Banten.

a reservoir to feed the baths of the Surosowan Palace; this was done by a canal tapped by four culverts which supplied the water.

Numerous finds have been made at Banten and collected in a small museum on the site. It contains fine Chinese porcelain from the eleventh to the nineteenth centuries, and curious terracotta interpretations of European motifs, notably the baskets of flowers and fruits made to decorate the Surosowan Palace.

Tirtayasa

The site of Tirtayasa, to the east of Banten, was the residence of Sultan Ageng at the end of the seventeenth century, and it was from this point that the Dutch attacked Banten.

The ruins are lost in modern constructions, but their interest lies in the fortifications (Fig. 12). Given the almost flat land around, these comprise a wall and a moat filled at all times by a stream. This only had to be dammed to turn the whole area into a marsh to thwart any attack. This, however, was not sufficient to deter Captain Tack, who led the Dutch army and took the town.

41

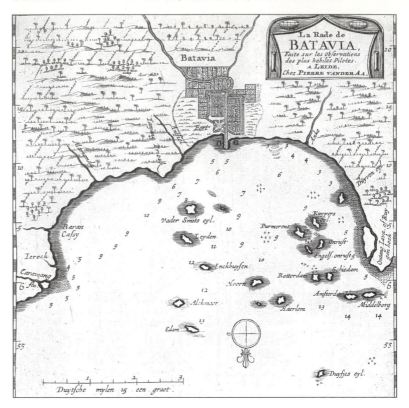

Fig. 13
The roads of Batavia according to the observations of the best pilots (Vander, *New Atlas*, Leiden, 1714).

Jakarta

The city was founded in the fourteenth century at which period it was a small port called Sunda Kelapa which supplied the Sundanese kingdom of Pajajaran until the sixteenth century, when it was conquered at the same time as Banten. At this juncture its name was changed to Jayakarta. No traces of this period remain except at Tugu, to the south of Priok. An inscription was found there dating from the seventh century deriving from Purnavarman, king of Taruma (the inscription is now in the National Museum). The first historical event which can be dated for certainty in this coastal region is the arrival of the Portuguese in 1522; they established friendly relations with the kingdom of Pajajaran. The first Dutch ships appeared here in 1596; the Dutch in 1610 obtained permission to build a warehouse which was transformed into a fort in 1618. The following year the Dutch destroyed the Muslim city and built on its site a new town, Batavia, which became the seat of the Dutch East India Company (the VOC).

In this period, Batavia occupied the left bank of the Ciliwong and was surrounded by a canal; the fort was on the right bank, close to the sea. The town spread at first to the east, and then, at the beginning of the eighteenth century, to the west (Fig. 13; on this map appear the names of the main subsequent extensions of the city in

42

the nineteenth and twentieth centuries; Tanjung Priok and Angkol to the east, and Angke to the west).

There are many remains of the eighteenth-century city. The Dutch overseers gave their buildings considerable unity, thanks to a style with a Javanese basis intermingled with European elements, essentially the architectural orders as they were described in Italian treatises of the end of the sixteenth century, above all, those of S. Serlio and A. Palladio (the latter was known through the English translation of Isaac Ware). This manner of building became entrenched and persisted until the end of the nineteenth century. The unity of these shapes conceals a great variety in plans; this is not special to Jakarta and is found, with variations, and better preserved, in

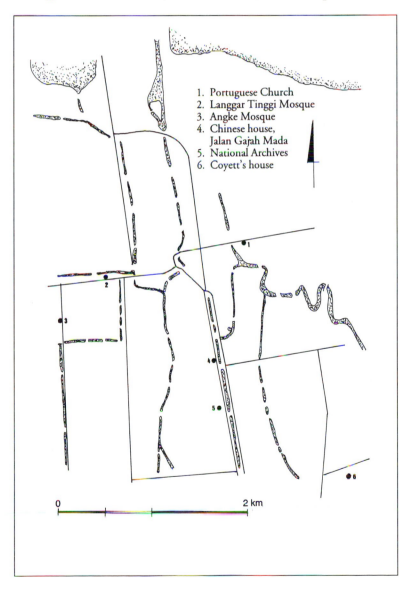

1. Portuguese Church
2. Langgar Tinggi Mosque
3. Angke Mosque
4. Chinese house,
   Jalan Gajah Mada
5. National Archives
6. Coyett's house

0   2 km

Fig. 14
Plan of the main monuments in Jakarta cited in the text.

Fig. 15
The present National Archives building in Jakarta seen from the rear garden.

Fig. 16.
Plan of Gunung Sari, Coyett's house, in Jakarta.

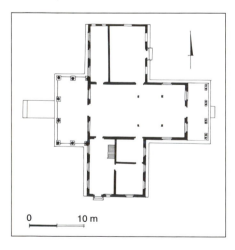

several Javanese towns, in particular in Pasuruan, which keeps its nineteenth-century appearance.

Outside Batavia rich merchants constructed huge residences which have now been swallowed up by the city (Fig. 14). This is the case of the mansion of Reiner de Klerk which now houses the Indonesian National Archives (Fig. 15; 5 in Fig. 14). The house known as Gunung Sari (38 Jalan Lautze, Fig. 16; 6 in Fig. 14) was built for a member of the Dutch East India Company, F. J. Coyett, who collected Indo-Javanese statues. He assembled a fair number which are still preserved in the house, which in 1762 became a Chinese temple, Klenteng Sentiong. This was a very large residence with an upper floor which was pulled down at the beginning of the nineteenth century (it still existed in 1813, the date of the drawing in Fig. 17). The western side was decorated with an Ionic portico inspired by Palladio, who also inspired the eastern portico with its Roman Doric order. This is the only one which can be seen today (Plate 20). Among the statues preserved in the temple is a very fine Durga from the beginning of the tenth century and a heavenly guardian which probably came from the temple of Singosari and dates from the thirteenth century.

Rich Chinese merchants towards the middle of the nineteenth century had houses built in the same districts which were externally

Fig. 17
Elevation of Coyett's house in Jakarta.

20. Present entrance porch of the
    Coyetts' house, Jakarta, with its
    Roman Doric order. (Jacques
    Dumarçay)

similar and sometimes with the same classical Palladian orders. Not far from the National Archives building is a very fine mansion (188 Jalan Gajah Mada) which conforms to the established model, but the interior is very different (4 in Fig. 14; Plate 21). There is no upper floor and no ceiling, and the very fine beamwork inside is exposed (Fig. 18). These architectural principles can also be seen in public and administrative buildings, mosques, and churches. In the Pekojan district, two mosques were built with façades decorated with classical orders. The recently destroyed mosque at Langgar Tinggi had a portico comprised of Tuscan columns doubtlessly inspired by a treatise by Serlio; the prayer room had ceilings, but outside under the porch, the beamwork was exposed and supported by Chinese consoles. The An Nawir Mosque was constructed using the Roman Doric order, probably designed in line with the same treatise. The so-called Portuguese Church (Fig. 19; 1 in Fig. 14; Plate 22), built in the very last years of the seventeenth century, also has resort to classical orders, using Roman Doric but in decorative woodwork, is of Chinese inspiration in the organ loft and the churchwardens' pen.

The administrative buildings constructed by the Dutch also employed these architectural principles. Thus the Town Hall completed in 1710 has a portico where two classical orders, Ionic and Roman Doric, are placed one above the other according to the

21. Roof of the Chinese house at 188 Jalan Gajah Mada, Jakarta. (Jacques Dumarçay)

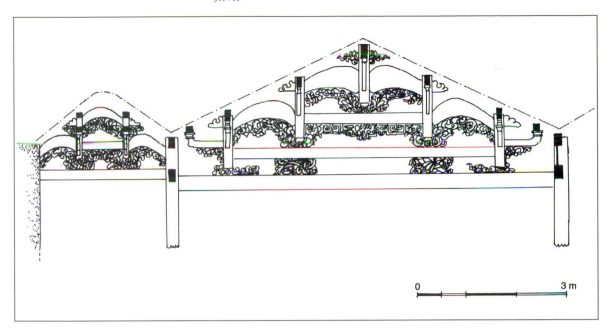

Fig. 18
Beamwork in the
Chinese house at 188
Jalan Gajah Mada,
Jakarta.

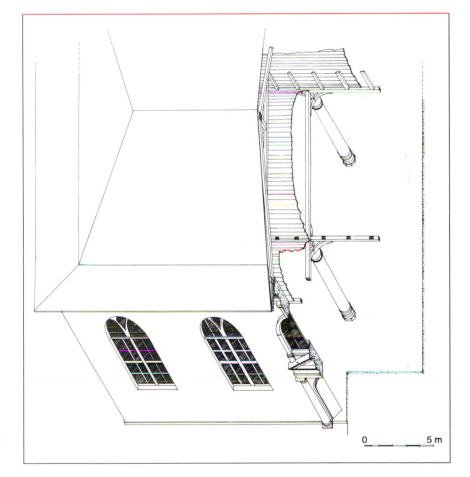

Fig. 19
Portuguese Church (1
in Fig. 14), built at the
end of the seventeenth
century in Jakarta.

22. Entrance to the Portuguese
Church, Jakarta. (Jacques
Dumarçay)

treatise of Palladio, and, even though a Dutch master carpenter was
employed, Chinese designs are found in the decoration of the staircases. The Town Hall has been turned into a Historical Museum of
the City of Jakarta.

The National Museum, built between 1862 and 1868, breaks
with this established pattern. Greek Doric was the model for the
principal entrance, which did not appear in the treatises used up to
this point. This museum has a very rich collection, not only in prehistoric objects and the classical period of Indo-Javanese art, but also
in ceramics (the collection of imported Chinese ceramics is particularly rich), and in objects concerning the ethnography of the whole
Indonesian archipelago.

Jakarta is, finally, the place where, in 1949, the representative of
the Netherlands recognized the independence of Indonesia after its
long anti-colonial struggle, and the name of the capital reverted to
its Javanese form.

Bandung
Bandung is one of the largest cities in Indonesia and its architectural
heritage, in spite of the inevitable losses that have occurred, remains

48

important. In particular, the Villa Isola, designed by the Dutch architect Schoemaker, is worthy of note. Following closely the precepts of his teacher, the architect J. Hoffman, Schoemaker in this large building was able to combine Javanese taste and concerns for blending the building into the landscape, and the Villa Isola follows the natural sweep of the land in its staircases. The Savoy Homann Hotel is also a good example of art deco architecture.

Cirebon

Cirebon is on the north coast of Java but, given the configuration of the coastline, faces east. The town and its port began to assume some importance only in the fourteenth century. The principality recognized the suzerainty of the Sultan of Demak at the beginning of the sixteenth century, but notwithstanding this, the town continued to constitute an independent state, maintaining relations with southern China, the states of South-East Asia, and the Middle East. The Dutch, at the beginning of the eighteenth century, installed a governor there, ending its independence.

There are numerous monuments of Cirebon's past in vast palaces, gardens, temples (Plate 23), and mosques. Among the latter is the grand mosque (Masjid Agung), one of the oldest in Java. Its orientation, which does not correspond to its surrounding wall, illustrates the debate which took place about orienting mosques precisely so that they conformed to the indications given in the Koran. The

23. Chinese temple in Cirebon. (Jacques Dumarçay)

49

masons had recourse to an apparition in the sky over the mosque in Mecca which the holy men who converted Java saw; the orientation thus indicated is roughly west (here it is 30 degrees to the north-west). When at the end of the nineteenth century more precise directives were given, the mosque at Cirebon was found to be correctly aligned and it is the surrounding wall which is no longer so.

Central Java

Semarang

Semarang is an intermediate point between Jakarta and Surabaya, and a port from where Magelang, Solo (Surakarta), and Yogyakarta were reached. But the town had very limited possibilities of development because the strip of land on which it is located between the sea and the mountains is extremely narrow.

Tradition has it that the Chinese admiral Cheng Ho disembarked at Semarang at the beginning of the fifteenth century; the Klenteng Cheng Ho recalls this event marked by a cement relief and a seventeenth century anchor found on the beach.

A Protestant Church was built in the town at the end of the eighteenth and the beginning of the nineteenth centuries that has a double dome which is unique in Java (Plate 24). Semarang

24. The dome of the Protestant Church in Semarang. (Jacques Dumarçay)

experienced considerable prosperity in the years 1920–5, and a number of buildings of this period give a very distinctive and solid character to the centre of the town.

One of the most interesting buildings in the art deco style is the Sobokarti Theatre built according to the plans of the architect T. Karsten. This combines European scenography with elements of Javanese architecture, in particular its beamwork (Karsten's models of beamwork were in fact already greatly influenced by Europe, though he did not realize this). The result is a most interesting building which fits in well with the urban setting of Semarang.

Dieng and Gedung Songo

These two sites, both first occupied in the eighth century, have many points in common: they are both located in the volcanic spine of central Java, Gedung Songo being near Ambarawa and Dieng (Colour Plate 1) close to Wonosobo. The latter site has been the subject of many excavations and studies, resulting in a good idea of the original state of the whole (Fig. 20).

The buildings found at Dieng are spread out at the edge and in the middle of an ancient depression, probably the remains of a crater, and close to a spring which feeds several small lakes. The most important group of temples is located in the middle of the depression; it comprises five (originally eight) small shrines, four of which, including Candi Puntadeva (Colour Plate 2; 4 in Fig. 20), face west and one, Candi Semar, east. The whole group is largely inspired by an Indian model, more particularly that of the southern Pallava dynasty, especially Candi Sembodro, which has a cruciform plan (Fig. 21). This is not the only source at Dieng though; Candi Bima, located at the edge of the depression (7 in Fig. 20), seems to follow a model probably deriving from Orissa, in northern India. The site was occupied over a long period of time; an inscription found there was carved in the thirteenth century and a small temple (3 in Fig. 20) dates from this time. Such a long occupancy led to all kinds of changes which are difficult to date precisely. A small section of the rock was dressed (5 in Fig. 20), a bathing place laid out (2 in Fig. 20), and above all a tunnel 4 metres in diameter was cut (to the south of the part of the site shown in Fig. 20) through the eastern edge of the crater.

The monuments reflect the history of the site; thus Candi Bima was built for Brahministic rites about 770, was taken over for Buddhist use about 800, at the time of Buddhism's greatest extension in Java, and reverted to Hinduism about 834.

The site of Gedung Songo (meaning nine buildings, but which now only number eight) is at the edge of a small valley formed by a stream. The basic model is found here of the Hindu shrines constructed elsewhere in Java and which was to have a marked success up to the end of the thirteenth century. It comprises a main temple with a lesser structure on either side, and with three annexes facing these, though sometimes there is only one annex, opposite the main temple. The complex here has considerable stylistic unity, and

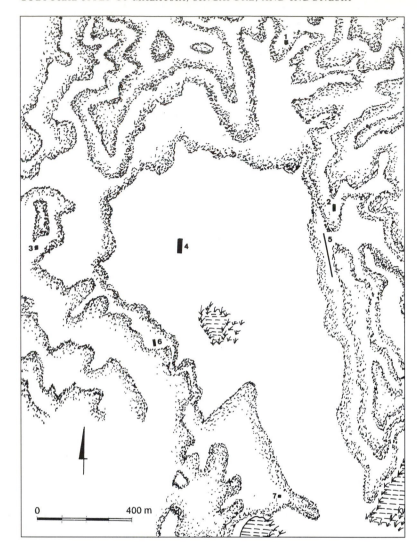

1. C. Dwarawati
2. Bathing place
3. Thirteenth-century
   temple
4. Pandava group
   of temples
5. Retaining wall
6. C. Gatokaca
7. C. Bima

Fig. 20
General plan of Dieng.

appears to have been built in the first half of the eighth century, with the exception of Candi I, which was probably constructed at the beginning of the ninth century.

Borobudur

The vast temple of Borobudur (Colour Plates 3–6) was laid out about 775, near the point where two rivers, the Progo and the Elo, join, and was probably selected in memory of the sacred conjunction of the Ganges and Yamuna rivers. The first builders made use of a hill which rises in the middle of a small depression. The first master mason was probably Hindu, working for one of the Sanjaya dynasty kings; he probably planned to alter the course of a small stream by building a canal which would have formed a pool around the monument.

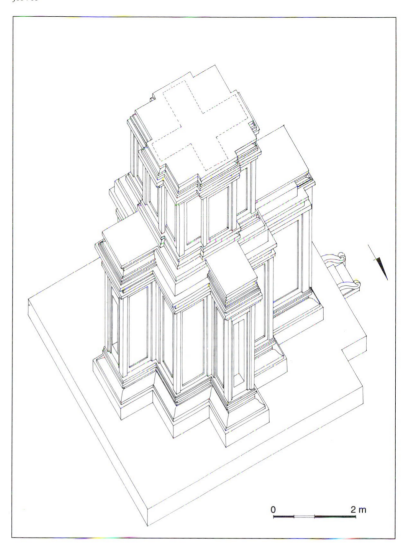

0   2 m

Fig. 21
Candi Sembodro (4 in Fig. 20) at
Dieng.

The site was also certainly selected on account of the large population which was found there. Before the restoration work was
recently undertaken, Professor Soekmono systematically explored
the site and a very large number of remains of villages was discovered
in the immediate environs of the main shrine. This was surrounded
by a huge enclosure, the corners of which were marked by temples;
only one of these has been discovered, Candi Waringen Putih, which
was laid out on the diagonal of Borobudur (Fig. 22). When, at the
end of the eighth century, the Buddhists of the Sailendra dynasty
reached the site, they could not allow such an obvious manifestation
of Shivaite power to remain, so they profoundly altered the monument, turning it into a shrine dedicated to the five Jina (Plate 25
shows the transformed upper terrace).

The Sailendra upsurge had its consequences throughout South-
East Asia, particularly in Cambodia, which at that time was under

53

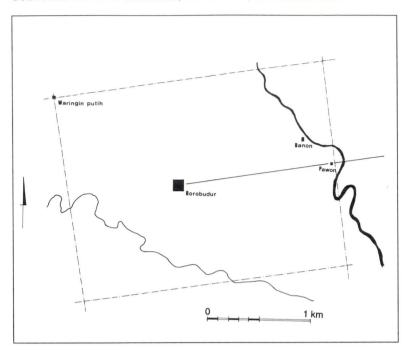

Fig. 22
Reconstitution of the perimeter of
Borobudur.

25. The upper terrace at Borobudur.
(Jacques Dumarçay)

54

Javanese Sanjaya suzerainty. The Sanjaya grip on power was considerably weakened by the Buddhist upsurge, and this allowed a Khmer prince to shake off Sanjaya domination; in 802 he became king, taking the name of Jayavarman II. This act did not eliminate Javanese influence, which appears in Khmer irrigation techniques and also in the layout of the Bakong at Roluos, which was largely inspired by the first state of Borobudur.

The transformation of the monument into a stupa gave it a duality which all scholars have stressed (Fig. 23). The modifications were not limited just to the main structure, but related temples, Candi Mendut (Plate 26) and Candi Pawon, which were originally built in brick, were completely covered with a stone facing.

If the monument did not lose its function with the Hindu revival in central Java around 830, this did not hold true for the entire site, for on the banks of the Progo a new temple, Candi Banon, dedicated to the Trimurti, was built.

Under UNESCO auspices, Borobudur was the object of a major restoration project which had the effect of re-emphasizing the broad horizontal lines of the monument's architectural concept.

Fig. 23
Axonometric perspective of Borobudur, from the north-east corner; the shadings represent the different periods of construction.

Yogyakarta

The Yogyakarta region played an important role in Javanese history in relation to its immediate neighbourhood of the major sites of

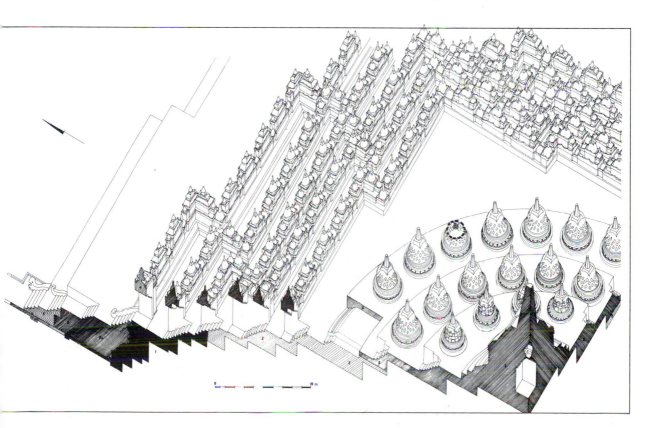

26. Statue of a Bodhisattva in Candi Mendut near Borobudur. (Jacques Dumarçay)

Borobudur and Prambanan. These, for reasons which are not entirely clear, lost their importance at the end of the ninth century and the focus of power shifted to the east of the island. It was only during the sixteenth century that the Yogyakarta region regained some importance which continued to grow with time.

At this period the sultans on the north coast of the island lost some of their influence to the centre. The royal Javanese epics (the *Babad*) attribute to the son of the last Majapahit king the foundation of a Muslim kingdom called Mataram, the capital of which was located at Kota Gede, on the eastern edge of the modern town. There are few vestiges of its past splendour; the tombs of Senopati, and some very late nineteenth- and early twentieth-century dwellings resulting from the trade in precious stones. Kota Gede

0   10m

Fig. 24
Axonometric view of the central part of
the garden of Warung Boto
(Rajawinangun), established from the
remaining ruins and a sketch by the
painter A. Payen in 1825.

played an important role in the Javanese War of 1825–30 between
Prince Diponegoro and the Dutch. On 18 July 1827 a violent battle
took place in which Diponegoro tried to take back Kota Gede from
the Dutch; the losses were considerable—more than 700 died on
one day.

Yogyakarta only became a true capital in the reign of Sultan
Mangkubumi (Hamengkubuwono I, r. 1755–92) after the division
of the kingdom of Mataram following fratricidal wars of succession.
The selection of the site was no easy matter. Once decided, the court
first stayed at Gamping, to the west of the city, while waiting for the
new palace to be built. Even though the new ruler was Muslim, the
name of the capital refers to Ayothya, the town where Rama reigned
victorious after overcoming the demons. The city is rich in remains
of its past, including the Sultan's palace (Colour Plates 7 and 8) and
numerous gardens (Fig. 24). Their foundation goes back to the reign

57

of Mangkubumi but the fighting of 1812 (in particular the seizure of the palace by the British on 20 June) caused considerable destruction, so that the monuments are largely in the condition in which restorations subsequent to 1814 left them.

Kerta and Plered

During the reign of Sultan Agung, the site of Kerta was selected in about 1615, probably because of the advantages for irrigation provided by the Opak River. The court moved to Kerta in 1618, but unfortunately a serious fire destroyed the palace in 1634, and today only the bases of a few columns remain (Plate 27). Sultan Agung decided to create a new capital close to Plered (Fig. 25). Work began in 1644 but the Sultan died two years later and his son Amangkurat I completed the construction the following year.

Amangkurat I was not content to build a new town, but he also completely changed the irrigation system by building a huge reservoir at Joho which was fed by the Opak. These works caused the river to change its course, and the town had to be protected by a dam, the Tambak, parallel to the new river bed. This was not high enough; in 1660, an exceptional flood caused the Opak to go around the Tambak dam and return to its original bed, and the decision to abandon Plered was taken. The move took place after the death of Amangkurat I in 1680.

Plered still had a part to play in the 1825–30 war, when Prince Diponegoro occupied the town and improved its defences. In April 1826 the Dutch tried to occupy the site, with only partial success. Their second attempt on 9 June the same year was entirely successful and constituted Diponegoro's first defeat.

27. The base of the *pendopo* of Sultan Agung's palace at Kerta. (Jacques Dumarçay)

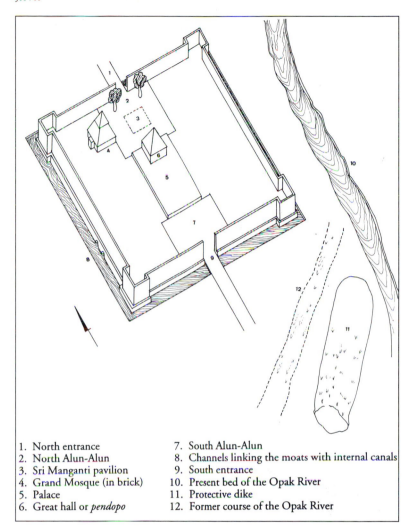

1. North entrance
2. North Alun-Alun
3. Sri Manganti pavilion
4. Grand Mosque (in brick)
5. Palace
6. Great hall or *pendopo*
7. South Alun-Alun
8. Channels linking the moats with internal canals
9. South entrance
10. Present bed of the Opak River
11. Protective dike
12. Former course of the Opak River

Fig. 25
General plan of Plered.

Candi Kalasan

This temple was the first Buddhist shrine in Java, and an inscription attests to its date of consecration in 775 (Colour Plate 9). In its first state, the shrine, dedicated to the goddess Tara, comprised a single square *cella* (sacred shrine area), but very soon, before the end of the eighth century, the temple was changed to serve the cult of the five Jina by the addition of a porch and three other *cellae*, which gives its present cruciform plan.

Candi Sari

This Buddhist shrine was built about 840 and is the only construction to survive in what was probably a very large complex, similar to that found at Plaosan. The shrine has six *cellae*, three on each of two floors; the upper level was reached by a wooden staircase, and the upper floor was likewise of wood. The richly decorated external façade does not correspond to the internal volume of two levels,

28. Candi Sari, near Prambanan.
(Jacques Dumarçay)

and the attic seen on the outside has no internal equivalent (Plate 28).

Prambanan

The site of Prambanan was probably selected about 750 by the Sailendra dynasty for the same reasons that, much later, Sultan Agung chose Kerta, namely the ease with which the Opak River lent itself to irrigation. The important inscription which describes the consecration of the great Shivaite temple at Prambanan in 856 mentions works carried out on the river; these were destroyed in a flood and much of the river bank was carried away, together with some of the outer shrines. The main temple compound has been extensively restored in recent years; the central shrine, dedicated to Shiva (Plate 29) and dominated internally by a huge statue of the god, is flanked to the north by Candi Brahma (Plate 30) and to the south by Candi Vishnu. Each is faced, to the east, by temples to the mounts of the gods, respectively the bull Nandin for Shiva, the mythical bird Garuda for Vishnu, and the goose Hamsa for Brahma. There are two other minor shrines in the central compound (Colour Plate 10), and 224 smaller shrines, the Candi Perwara, around. The shrines to the three Hindu gods are richly decorated, and also have important bas-reliefs.

60

29. Candi Shiva, decoration at
    Prambanan. (Jacques Dumarçay)

30. Candi Brahma and Candi Shiva at
    Prambanan. (Jacques Dumarçay)

Candi Sewu and Candi Plaosan

The Sailendra town around Prambanan is no longer discernible, but numerous religious buildings remain. The largest, Candi Sewu, has a complicated history which varies with the evolution of Buddhism in Java, and in a sense is an expression of its expansion. When the reaction of the Hindus came about, from 830, they were tolerant, neither changing the architecture nor banning the religion. But they built, close to Candi Sewu (Colour Plates 11 and 12), an enormous Shivaite complex which was to be the centre of a town, traces of which have been discovered in the small shrines marking its corners. This town was not oriented to the east like the main temple, the surrounding walls of which are not concentric.

In this Hindu town, at the same time, and consequently under the same king, an enormous Buddhist temple, Candi Plaosan (Colour Plates 13 and 14), was built, the laying out of which, like that of Candi Prambanan, is an expression of the kingdom in the form of a vast mandala (Plates 31 and 32).

The architectural remains of this site are considerable. They are not all purely religious. A palace complex, Ratu Boko, was built on a

31. Candi Plaosan, near Prambanan: the main sanctuary. (Jacques Dumarçay)

32. Candi Plaosan, near Prambanan: a secondary shrine. (Jacques Dumarçay)

hill overlooking the temples (Plate 33). However, perhaps because of a natural disaster or the destruction of a dam on the Opak, the site of Prambanan was abandoned by the rulers, who moved to the east of the island. The temples continued to be centres of worship; inscriptions were engraved in the region until the end of the eleventh century, then the temples were pillaged. The temple of Sambisari (Colour Plate 15) well illustrates this; after being abandoned and pillaged, it was covered with ash from a volcanic eruption, and the persons who in recent times excavated it found the base of a linga lying on its side, leaving the foundation well open; of course the foundation deposit, usually of gold, had disappeared.

Kartasura

The move from Plered after the Joho dam gave way in 1660 did not, in fact, take place for another twenty years. The new site selected, Kartasura, was just as favourable for establishing irrigation works, but less exposed to floods. The remains of this town are today of little importance, and comprise a few buildings which were probably the foundations of the palace.

62

33. The main entrance to Kraton Ratu Boko. (Jacques Dumarçay)

Surakarta (Solo)

The establishment of the successor capital Surakarta has been described in detail in a long account, the *Babad Giyanti*, which covers events in the second half of the eighteenth century in central Java. The choice of the new site was the object of all kinds of competitions, in particular those of soothsayers. In spite of the marshy ground, the auspices for future prosperity carried the day, and on 20 February 1745 the city was founded (this date, though, does not appear to be the correct one; another tradition maintains it was 9 February 1756).

In its original layout the town plan was cruciform, with the sultan's palace prolonged to the north and the south by two vast squares. By the end of the eighteenth century the Great Mosque was completed, as well as the new Dutch fort, the Vastenburg. Given its location, the town was often flooded; in the reign of Sultan Pakubuwono IV (1788–1820), major public works were undertaken to shift the course of the Bengawan River to the east. It was especially from the time of the reign of this ruler that the town's prosperity began, thanks to it being able to attract a considerable number of Chinese merchants.

The monuments of Surakarta are those connected with its rulers, and essentially their palaces. The largest is that of Kraton Hadiningrat, in the centre of the town. Unfortunately, it suffered a

63

34. Candi Sukuh, on Mount Lawu.
    (Jacques Dumarçay)

35. Candi Ceto, on Mount Lawu.
    (Jacques Dumarçay)

serious fire in 1985. The Kraton Mangkunegoro, belonging to a lesser branch of the royal family which, nevertheless, in theory had its own separate state from 1757, is more impressive, and integrates very satisfactorily traditional Javanese buildings with modern additions designed by the Dutch architect T. Karsten. It also has an important collection of artefacts.

To the east of Surakarta, high on the slopes of Mount Lawu, are two very late temples of the Majapahit period, Candi Sukuh (Plate 34), *c*.1430, in the form of a truncated pyramid on three terraces, with erotic carvings in its entrance pavilions, and Candi Ceto (Plate 35), *c*.1470, in the form of seven much restored terraces originally housing wooden pavilions.

Demak

The small town of Demak, numbering barely 10,000 inhabitants, is located inland at the foot of the Jepara peninsula. The first Muslim sultanate was formed here, and from this town Islam spread throughout Java. The most ancient mosque found on the island, dating from the sixteenth century, is located here (Fig. 26). The building is directly inspired by Majapahit architecture, with a square *pendopo* (pavilion), each side 20 metres long, covered with three roof levels resting on radiating beamwork (Fig. 27). The call to prayer

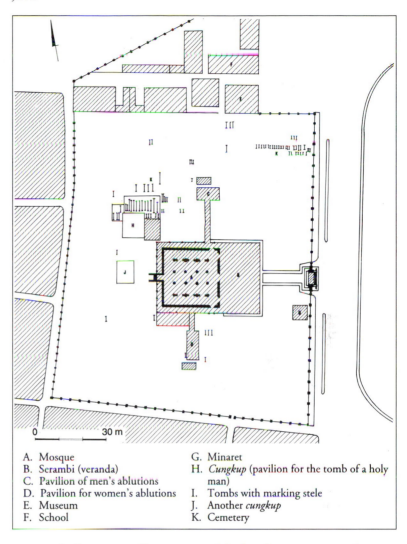

A. Mosque
B. Serambi (veranda)
C. Pavilion of men's ablutions
D. Pavilion for women's ablutions
E. Museum
F. School

G. Minaret
H. *Cungkup* (pavilion for the tomb of a holy man)
I. Tombs with marking stele
J. Another *cungkup*
K. Cemetery

Fig. 26
Plan of the mosque compound at Demak.

was made from a small room set aside for the purpose at the top, beneath the roof. The orientation of the building is the subject of pious legends: 'How shall we know the right direction?' the holy Sunan Giri is said to have asked, and received the reply from Sunan Kalijaya: 'Let us pray and we shall know.' They closed their eyes to pray and when they opened them the Kaaba of Mecca was reflected in the sky, which allowed them to determine the correct direction, to the west. In the nineteenth century, an imam, in spite of the legend, corrected this mythical orientation with a more precise one.

The mosque was profoundly changed in the nineteenth century with the addition of a masonry wall to enclose the *pendopo*, a ceiling concealing the beamwork, and above all a mihrab indicating the direction of Mecca. While these transformations were being carried out, a minaret with a metal roof-frame was built in the courtyard. Recently the mosque has again been entirely reconditioned, particularly in regard to the four central pillars and the roof tiles.

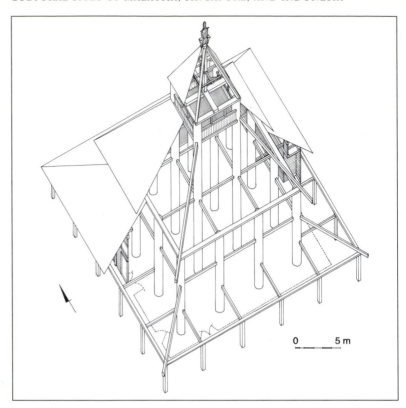

Fig. 27
Reconstitution of the original form of
the mosque at Demak.

At Jepara, close to Demak, was a mosque, now completely
destroyed, which was legendary. It is described as having five superposed roofs, which must have made it similar to a very large Balinese
meru (a tower used for offerings).

East Java

Majapahit

The site of the ancient capital of the kingdom of Majapahit, which
flourished from the end of the thirteenth century to 1478, when it
fell to Muslim Demak, is located near the village of Trowulan,
between Madiun and Surabaya in East Java. Today, it is an immense
stretch of ruins, some of which are still discernible or have been
restored.

There have been many attempts to reconstitute the Majapahit
town; the most plausible is perhaps that of the architect Maclaine
Pont, who suggested a vast cruciform enclosure comprising not only
the architectural remains but also a considerable area which was set
aside for agriculture (Fig. 28). Recently, following aerial photo-
graphs, archaeologists have suggested there was a vast complex of
canals intersecting each other at right angles. This seems scarcely
probable; these lines were more likely old brickfields. Not only has
the site been pillaged by treasure hunters and more recently by

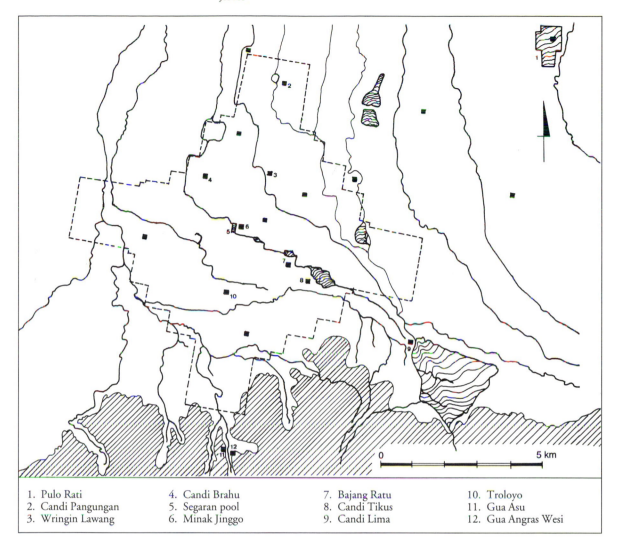

Fig. 28
Plan of the site of Majapahit.

1. Pulo Rati
2. Candi Pangungan
3. Wringin Lawang
4. Candi Brahu
5. Segaran pool
6. Minak Jinggo
7. Bajang Ratu
8. Candi Tikus
9. Candi Lima
10. Troloyo
11. Gua Asu
12. Gua Angras Wesi

people simply looking for bricks, so that sometimes the city walls appear in reverse, the trenches of the plunderers following the layout of the walls, but also, when this resource was exhausted, new bricks had to be made, which was done on the spot, the soil of the area being very good for terracotta production.

The town lay beside a small mountainous outcrop where several caves, the Gua Asu and Gua Angras Wesi, for example, were turned into hermitages (11 and 12 in Fig. 28). The mountain also provided the water source for the town; all the small streams coming down from it were utilized in the town's hydraulic system. The best known of these works is the dam retaining a large area of water near the small temple Candi Lima (9 in Fig. 28). Another less important construction is found near the bathing place of Candi Tikus (8 in Fig. 28), for which it provided water. The large and well-known reservoir of Segaran (5 in Fig. 28) has sometimes been compared to a Khmer *baray*, a man-made reservoir, but it neither utilizes the same techniques (the Segaran pool is dug out of the ground, whereas the *baray* were built on the level of the land), nor comprises comparable dimensions—the Western Baray at Angkor, for example, was 7 kilometres in length, Segaran only 300 metres.

The main architectural remains are for the most part built of brick, with occasionally some stone elements. These structures are scattered over the site without any overall plan being apparent. The great gate Wringin Lawang (3 in Fig. 28) appears as a massive temple which has been sliced into two separate parts; the threshold of the gate is raised and reached by two stairways. It is no longer possible today to distinguish the interior from the exterior of the complex on to which Wringin Lawang gave access. Another gateway on a smaller scale, but more complete and better preserved, Bajang Ratu (7 in Fig. 28), has recently been given careful restoration. Like Wringin Lawang, this gate comprises a temple, but instead of being divided into two separate parts, the master builder linked it with a single element over the entrance. The doorway is particularly narrow, being little more than one metre wide after the positioning of the door frames, which implies an entrance to a temple. The composition is rounded off on either side of the central part with two false doorways like those giving access to the upper level of the great temple at Prambanan. These throwbacks to earlier structures show how much the master masons, in spite of the novelty of their structures, preserved the spirit of classical works.

Candi Brahu (4 in Fig. 28) is a brick temple whose main façade has collapsed, revealing the internal cantilever. Candi Tikus (9 in Fig. 28) is a bathing place, but different from those of Jalatunda and Belahan in that it is built on the plain, and though the structure comprises the same elements as the others, they are disposed differently. Water was brought to this bathing place through a large structure probably representing Mount Meru, and appears to flow under it through channels feeding the water spouts, and the two tanks where the ritual ablutions were performed which face the central structure. Waste water was taken away on the same side as these tanks.

Candi Jawi

This temple (Colour Plate 16) was built at the end of the thirteenth century during the reign of King Kertanagara (1268–92), who believed in the profound unity of Buddhism and Shivaism, so the main statue in the temple shows half of Shiva and half of the Buddha Aksobaya. This syncretism is also shown in the architecture; the base of the monument is decorated with reliefs of Hindu inspiration, and the topmost part is in the form of a stupa. This temple unusually also has preserved most of its moats and enclosure walls. Its overall plan, with its successive courtyards and their entrance doorways, exercised much influence on Balinese architecture, as at Mengwi, for example, where not only are the same enclosures found but also the internal moat.

Candi Belahan

This comprises a huge group of structures, the principal remains being those of the enclosures and the bathing place. This has only one tank for ablutions, and the water was brought behind a masonry block with two niches hollowed out for the statues of the wives of the god Vishnu. One has water issuing from her hands, the other from her breasts.

Penanggungan

Mount Penanggungan (Fig. 29; Plate 36) has the same outline as the descriptions of the legendary Mount Meru, a peak surrounded by

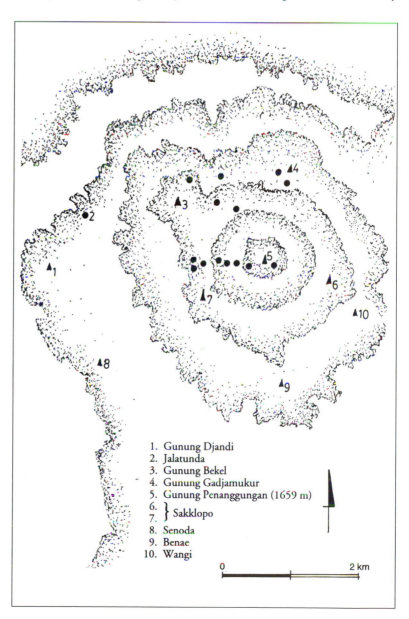

1. Gunung Djandi
2. Jalatunda
3. Gunung Bekel
4. Gunung Gadjamukur
5. Gunung Penanggungan (1659 m)
6. } Sakklopo
7. }
8. Senoda
9. Benae
10. Wangi

0   2 km

Fig. 29
Contour plan of Mount Penanggungan, the natural Mount Meru.

36. Mount Penanggungan with the natural shape of Mount Meru. (Jacques Dumarçay)

four outcrops, so the small natural peak, reaching 1659 metres in its central part, was arranged as a dwelling place for the gods from the beginning of the fifteenth century. The oldest inscription on the mountain dates from 1404, but it is likely that Mount Penanggungan was used as a sacred mountain before that date, since it appears in the background of one of the reliefs decorating the base of Candi Jawi at the end of the thirteenth century, and the bathing place of Jalatunda was established at the foot of the mountain in the tenth century.

The gods on Meru inhabit caves arranged to suit their needs. The small temples on the slopes of Mount Penanggungan reproduce this arrangement. For example, Candi Putri is built on the side of the slope and has three successive terraces reached by an axial stairway leading to the top. A simple wall built against the rock sheltered the statue of the god.

Temple LXV is even closer to the legendary model, for after different terraces a small enclosure surrounded by high walls gives on to a natural cave which is the home of the god.

Jalatunda

The bathing place of Jalatunda (2 in Fig. 29) was built of stone at the base of Mount Penanggungan on its western flank at the end of the tenth century and was remodelled in the thirteenth century. It comprises a central mass built against a retaining wall embedded into the mountain and concealing the water source. Nine jets cut into the rock, in the shape of nine linga, released the water which fell into a pool from which it escaped through gargoyles. On either side of the water source were tanks for ritual ablutions which had their own water sources; to avoid an excess of water, overflow tanks were provided. In the thirteenth century, these arrangements were altered; superficially, the decoration was entirely renewed, with the addition of vertically ranked gargoyles and structures in the form of mountains.

Candi Pari

This building is not far from the town of Porong, and must have formed part of a group of shrines of which Sumur and Pamotan were part. The temple bears the date equivalent to 1371 on the lintel over its entrance; it is built of brick with some stone elements. The entrance beneath the lintel has carved into the brick a building showing its roof beamwork in tension. This picture lacks any architectural significance, and is only there to show the temple was dedicated to Vishnu, for Sri, one of Vishnu's wives, was the goddess protecting rice cultivation, and rice was stored in granaries whose roofs had sagging ridges.

Singosari

Singosari is the site of the capital of the kingdom at the time of King Hayam Waruk. The town was destroyed in 1298, but there are still important remains, including those of the main temple, a section of the ramparts, and one of the city gates with statues of its guardians. The site was the object of an important survey conducted by Leydie Melville, and the restoration of the main temple was completed by the Archaeological Department in 1936.

The restoration work also revealed other buildings called simply Candi A–E (E is also sometimes known as Candi Wayang); there were in addition three other temples, Candi F–H, about which almost nothing is known.

The main temple (Colour Plate 17; Plate 37) has a cruciform plan and is built on a base with sides 14 metres long; on the west was a platform which has now disappeared and which led into the temple proper. On three other sides are placed in projection a shrine for the lesser divinities, Agastya, Ganesha, and Durga, following the iconography established in the eighth century in central Java (as at Prambanan, for example). Above this level is a tower similar to that at Candi Kidal but with four false doorways. In the temple courtyard statues representing the guardians of the universe were found (Plate 38). It is likely that these statues indicate a change in the layout of the temple; the points from which the builders took their dimensions were no longer replaced by small linga as before but by these statues to the guardians of the universe.

The other structures are now swallowed up by the modern town, but these remains are of considerable interest and indicate the extent of the ancient site.

Penataran

The different inscriptions carved on the monuments here give an idea of the length of time it took to build them; the earliest dates from 1347 and the most recent 1375. Thus twenty-eight years were

37. The main temple at Singosari. (Jacques Dumarçay)

38. The giant guardian on the west gate of Singosari. (Jacques Dumarçay)

39. The dated temple of Penataran.
(Jacques Dumarçay)

required to construct these relatively simple structures, showing to what extent the religious impulse had been lost; only twenty-four years were required in the ninth century to build the enormous ensemble of Prambanan.

Penataran (Plate 39), is built on sloping ground next to a stream which supplies water to several bathing places connected with the temple. The master builder utilized the slope in his overall plan, dividing the area into successively rising terraces up to the bank of the stream.

The buildings appear to be of stone, but for the most part stone is only used as a facing on a brick core; this allows for easier carving in relief. The very rich decoration illustrates Indian epics, notably the *Ramayana*, the scenes of which have often been compared to those found at Prambanan. The base of the temple is decorated with winged lions; the dwelling of the god here is a flying palace revolving around Mount Meru.

72

Candi Jago

Today, this temple, built in 1280, is found surrounded by the town of Tumpang. It comprises a massive base on three levels decorated with remarkable reliefs. A Buddhist shrine was formerly at the top.

Candi Kidal

This temple (Plate 40), built in 1260, is found not far from Tumpang; it was formerly most probably the central point of a vast ensemble of buildings. Candi Kidal was a Vishnuite temple, and in the reliefs found on its base can be seen Garuda carrying a snake, Garuda bearing the vase containing the liquor of immortality, and Garuda carrying Laksmi, as well as the myth of the churning of the sea of milk during which, accidentally, the world was created. The gods and demons, having lost their immortality, combined to seek out the liquor which would allow them to regain it. Having learnt that this precious juice was hidden under Mount Mandara, they took from the bottom of the ocean a giant snake which they

40. Candi Kidal, near Tumpang, Java. (Jacques Dumarçay)

wrapped around the mountain and alternately pulled on it, causing the mountain to move and the liquor to flow from the mountain, as well as all kinds of fabulous beings and feminine divinities, the first being Laksmi, who at once became the wife of Vishnu. The churning created concentric waves and fragments of butter which floated on the ocean. These elements accidentally formed our world and remained in position once the gods and demons ceased their churning. This moment is shown at Candi Kidal; the temple becomes Mount Mandara raised in the middle of a slightly sloping courtyard which could be filled with water representing the ocean, the lumps of no longer floating butter are the surrounding shrines, and the enclosure represents the first wave to reach the mountain. It seems likely that there were other concentric enclosures representing immobilized waves, to a maximum of seven.

This representation of the universe shows the degree to which Javanese kings remained in contact with other South-East Asian states, especially with the Khmer kingdom of Jayavarman VII (1181–1219), whose city of Angkor was likewise a representation of the creation of the world. In this optic Vishnu was not only the creator of the world but also its first universal king; Javanese kings attempted to model themselves on this role from the beginning of the kingdom and to transform themselves into a manifestation of Vishnu on earth, as the ambitious claims of the inscriptions show.

Candi Badut

This temple was constructed in the end of the eighth century when the centre of power was still in Central Java. It is very similar to the temples found at Dieng but notably wider. The interesting part about the structure are the changes made to it. The first was made in the ninth century when the ritual required the central space to be free of other structures. Candi Badut, being built right in the middle, the master mason decided to reconstruct the surrounding enclosure with a new layout leaving the centre free. In the thirteenth century, during another refashioning, the false storeys of the tower were entirely changed, as well as the upper part, and the approach to the tower.

Surabaya

Surabaya is the most important port in Java, but because of its increasing prosperity its buildings were rapidly renewed, and there are few traces of its early architecture. The city has neither the unity of Pasuran (below) nor its monumental refinement. Yet the Chinese quarter of the city has a great number of houses with roofs utilizing Chinese beamwork and decoration. Many of these have multiple brackets superposed one above the other in two, three or more levels.

Pasuran

This town has today lost much of its influence but in the sixteenth century was still inhabited by people of Hindu persuasion. It became

74

important at the beginning of the nineteenth century when sugar mills were set up near by, and the city had 38,000 inhabitants. Because it grew very rapidly, its architecture shows great homogeneity, and forms a classical style inspired by Palladio and Serlio, whose treatises were known in Jakarta, but with Javanese roofs. There are some exceptions to the overall unity; for example, the Catholic church was built in 1895 in an Italian Gothic style with a curious mixture in its entrance portico of Corinthian columns and pointed arches; the nave is lit by ogival windows filled with stained glass.

The Harmony Club had built, for its centre, a large Palladian building, with a very imposing entrance decorated with Ionic columns and a theatre.

In the Chinese quarter, houses were built in the 1920s which appear to be European, but which incorporated interesting ceramic details or very Javanese pinnacle turrets.

Candi Gunung Gansir

This temple was at first, because of its stylistic appearance, thought to date from the ninth century, but it seems in reality, given its plan and the architectural techniques used, that it was built in the fourteenth century. The chief interest of the shrine and its decoration are in its use of graphic perspectives, for example, in the decoration above the niches showing the summit of a temple but indicating that it was a representation and not a real temple; carved birds were added to give the scale.

Candi Jabung

Candi Jabung (Fig. 30; Plates 41 and 42) is a Buddhist temple located in a very large enclosure, the corners of which are marked by small solid structures, the Candi Sudut (only that in the south-west corner is well preserved). The date of construction, corresponding to 1354, is carved in the lintel of the entrance doorway. The base is square, with a projecting and very steep straight stairway to the west. The temple proper is externally circular, which is quite exceptional in Java, and the inside constitutes a *cella* with an octagonal plan. It is difficult to imagine how the upper part of the temple looked, but it was most likely a stupa with a projecting relief on each of the axes.

Blambangan

Blambangan (Banyuwangi), located at the easternmost point of Java, was a tiny state which remained Hindu until the end of the seventeenth century. From the beginning of the fifteenth century a civil war broke out between Majapahit and Blambangan, and gradually the principality of Blambangan asserted its independence, achieving it in 1478.

There are few sites associated with this state and many of the remains known from travellers' engravings (in particular those of J. Th. Bik) have been destroyed. The most important remaining site is of Macan Putih, which was probably a town surrounded by an

41. Candi Jabung, a Buddhist temple in
    East Java. (Jacques Dumarçay)

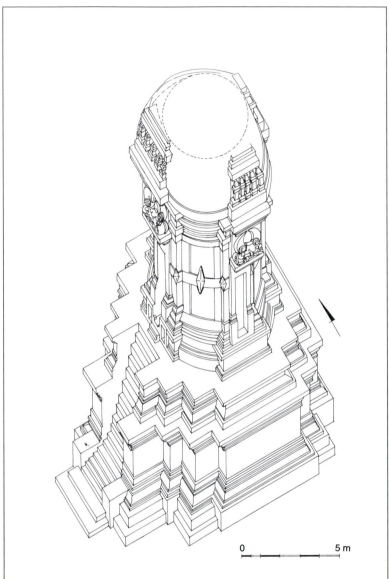

0   5 m

Fig. 30
Axonometric drawing of Candi Jabung.

42. Close-up of Candi Jabung. (Jacques Dumarçay)

impressive enclosure 4.50 kilometres in perimeter and built of brick. To the east was a temple, facing west, built on a giant turtle or a kind of dragon, if the drawings Bik are to be believed. Although inscriptions found are very brief, it was probably a temple built to mark the churning of the sea of milk when Vishnu, in the form of a turtle, slid under Mount Meru to assist in moving the mountain.

Java, from Banten to Blambangan, is a place where architecture is privileged, a land where buildings play a role independent of the symbolic or historic meaning. Borobudur is the best example; at first conceived as a Hindu temple, then Buddhist, with a great number of different explanations, and is today considered a kind of Indonesian palladium, without its architectural space being profoundly modified. This can also be seen in the construction of mosques espousing the form of the *pendopo,* a structure conceived during the Majapahit dynasty with no connections with Islam, but which integrates perfectly with the Javanese countryside.

5   Bali and Lombok

THE cultural sites of Bali are extremely numerous, and almost every village has its own rich traditions, its paintings, carvings, music, and ancient texts; here only an outline will be given of a cultural ensemble which is, on any count, quite exceptional. Its sister island to the east, Lombok, parts of which were long under Balinese occupation, will also be considered in this chapter.

Bali

Pejeng

Bali is located to the east of Java and its art owes much to Javanese civilization, especially to the Majapahit period (thirteenth to sixteenth centuries), many elements of which have been preserved in Bali. But Bali was inhabited in prehistoric times, and the remains of this early period are of great importance. The most famous is the bronze drum, dating from about the third century BC, at Pejeng, and known as the 'Moon of Pejeng'. Its upper surface area is 1.6 metres in diameter, which is so big that it is thought it must have been cast in Bali, even though it is clearly related to the bronze drums of the Dong Son civilization. The Moon of Pejeng is now kept in the Pura Penataran Sasih temple of the Intaran palace in the Gianyar district, in a pavilion which makes it difficult to see and appreciate its dimensions and its detail.

Goa Gajah

It is possible that before absorbing Javanese influences, Bali was in direct contact with Indian culture. When the Chinese traveller I-Tsing visited Bali in 670, he placed the island in the regions converted to Buddhism. Sites exist where Buddhism was practised at very early dates, like those around Lake Bratan, but the first historic evidence dates from the eighth to the tenth centuries, probably already mixed with some Javanese influences. Close to the site of Goa Gajah can be seen the remains of a Buddhist monastery, Arca Buddha, unfortunately in a very ruined condition, but with a seated Buddha statue which can be dated to the ninth century. The statue placed beneath a pavilion in front of the cave of Goa Gajah probably represents Hariti, and came from this monastery. Hariti was an ogress who ate children and who after being converted to Buddhism became their protectress.

It was in Sanur that the first inscription written in Sanskrit and Old Balinese was found, and in which a king ruling an island is mentioned. It was carved on a pillar which probably formed part of the palace of the ruler Adipatih (meaning king) Sri Kesari Varuma. The end of the inscription has been effaced, though the date, equivalent to 914 AD, remains.

After this date, an increasing number of remains is found. The site of Goa Gajah (Colour Plate 18) comprises a large bathing place separated by two pools filled with water coming from spouts in vases supported by female statues, three for each pool. Archaeologists have related this bathing place to that at Belahan in Java, which dates from the eleventh century in its final form. The six statues in the bathing place are aligned to the entrance to the cave which gives its name to the site (meaning Elephant Cave). The interior of the cave is T-shaped; there are two chambers with niches in the vertical bar, and in the horizontal bar are eleven niches hollowed into the walls; in some there are Shivaite linga. The entrance to the cave is surmounted by a monster's head surrounded by a large relief showing in a stylized manner a mountain with its hermit and animal dwellers and imaginary scenes.

Gunung Kawi

The magnificent site of Gunung Kawi comprises three distinct groups; the kings' tombs, the queens' tombs, and the monastery. The royal tombs (more properly memorials, since neither the bodies nor the ashes were placed here) are cut into the volcanic tuff cliff in the shape of massive though small temples. Above the frame of one of the tombs the date equivalent to 1079 is carved in relief. This form is similar to the structure of temples in East Java (thus before being influenced by Java, Bali in some degree influenced the designs of Javanese master masons). These architectural groups are lined up on a terrace in which was hollowed out before each of the false shrines a structure containing a rock divided into nine sections, in each of which would have been placed precious stones and metal objects, perhaps representing the spirit of the dead person, whose body would have been burnt and the ashes cast into the sea. Only one of these stones remains in position, in the group of the queens' tombs, which are to the left of the site on arriving down the numerous steps leading to and before crossing the river.

The monastery of Gunung Kawi, located near the royal tombs, is likewise hewn out of living rock and reproduces as closely as possible wooden structures showing, amongst other things, the oldest form of beamwork known, without hip-rafters, still today used in Bali and Java. To the right of this monastery is another group, probably of the same form, where the monks' cells cut into the rock are divided into two parts, the one in front acting as a resting place, and the other for meditation. This last group is similar to the monastery of Kalebutan near Pejeng, where beside the river bed a false shrine has been carved. The buildings comprising this monastery are spread over two levels and are in a very ruined condition.

Besakih

Although the temple at Besakih has been rebuilt many times, it remains one of the oldest foundations in Bali. Its construction may possibly have been ordered by King Kesari mentioned in the Sanur inscription. In the fifteenth century the King of Gegel transformed the shrine into a temple to his ancestors. The site was largely spared the terrible 1963 eruption of Gunung Agung (3142 metres), on the southern slopes of which it is built, adding to the sanctity of the place. It forms a very large complex 950 metres above the surrounding plain, with structures on six main terraces ranged on a northeasterly alignment. Most of the buildings are recent, since the site, exposed to all the monsoon winds, is not conducive for wooden structures to last long. The main buildings are dedicated to Shiva, and are flanked to the right and left with two annexes of lesser importance but built on parallel axes to the Shivaite temple, and dedicated to Brahma and Vishnu.

Bangli

Not far from Besakih, on the road from Gianyar in the south to Penelokan and Lake Batur, lies Bangli, which at one stage was the capital of the whole island. Bangli has one of the finest temples in Bali, the Pura Kehan (Colour Plate 19; Plate 43). A vast flight of stairs leads to the main entrance to the temple and the outer courtyard. The inner temple contains an eleven-tier *meru* tower and shrine to the Hindu Trimurti.

Tampaksiring

The bathing place of Tirtha Empul near Tampaksiring is an ancient site dating from the tenth century which has been restored recently—by the gods, according to legend. The most interesting part of the site is its pools fed by springs forming part of the headwaters of the Pakerisan River. The site remains very popular for the inhabitants of Gianyar, for whom it is particularly sacred.

From the fifteenth century Majapahit influences became stronger and it is likely that it was in this period that architectural forms became fixed since they appeared to have pleased the gods; building manuals then began to be compiled. These treatises establish norms, and could have stifled architectural invention, which happened to some extent in India; but in Bali nothing of the kind occurred, and the manuals were constantly updated, incorporating new techniques and technologies. The most recent, for example, include methods of using reinforced concrete. There remain, though, in these manuals, indications of their ancient origins: for example, it is recommended not to give the same height to all the doors of a temple. This is indeed the case at Candi Kidal in East Java, where the main door has a height of 1.92 metres while the side doors are only 1.85 metres high. What caused the Balinese masons to be more inventive was the indifferent materials with which they worked; their bricks are poorly

43. Entrance to the Pura Kehan at Bangli, Bali. (Jacques Dumarçay)

fired, volcanic tuff easily crumbles, and wood is attacked by insects. It was therefore necessary frequently to renew their very fragile buildings.

Mengwi

The temple at Mengwi (Fig. 31), one of the stakes in the internal Balinese wars at the end of the nineteenth century, is 15 kilometres to the north of Denpasar. It resembles in many respects the layout of temples in East Java (for example, Candi Jawi). The Mengwi shrine (Colour Plate 20), properly known as the Pura Sada of Kapal, comprises three main levels. The middle and lower ones are partially

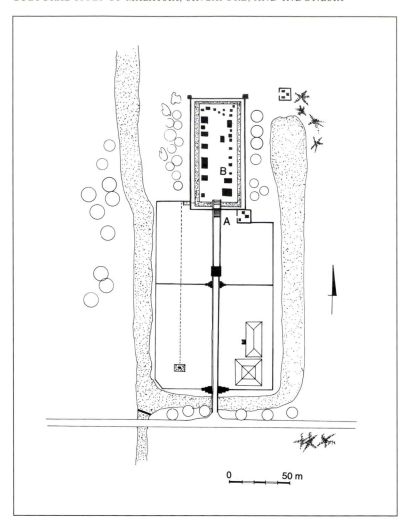

Fig. 31
Plan of the whole shrine of Mengwi,
Bali.

surrounded by the branches of a small stream fed by a retaining dam
acting as a moat on three sides of the site. This dam plays an important part in the irrigation of the nearby rice fields, and was a source
of conflict when the inhabitants of the villages dependent on the
temple converted to Christianity; they were considered dead to
Hinduism and were not allowed to share in the waters deriving from
the temple. This dam was used during the last war under the
Japanese occupation to generate electricity.

The upper level of the temple has a retaining wall with only
one gateway, facing south. Within the enclosure is a ditch fed by
the stream completely surrounding the terrace; it is crossed by a
bridge in front of the south-facing gate. The outlet for this ditch is in
the south-west corner from where an underground conduit feeds the
small pool in the middle level. In the centre of this pool is shown
the churning of the sea of milk in the Hindu myth of the creation of
the world (Colour Plate 21). This middle level is also surrounded by

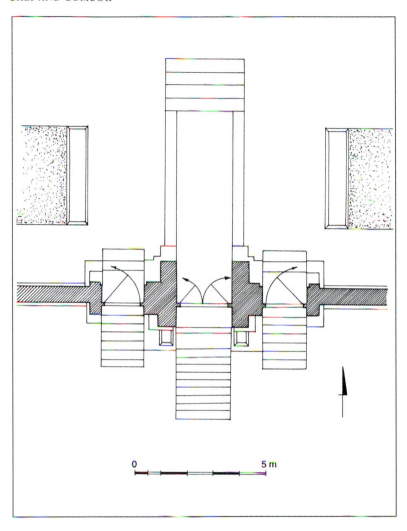

Fig. 32
Plan of the entrance to the inner
enclosure of the temple
of Mengwi (A in Fig. 31), Bali.

an enclosing wall divided into two unequal parts. Visitors from one
to the other pass through a monumental split gateway (Fig. 32).
This wall does not go around that of the upper terrace; to the east it
joins a building marking the south-east corner of the upper terrace
containing the hollowed-out tree-trunks used for sounding the
alarm (*kulkul*). To the west the enclosure ends with the outlet of
the ditch. This layout gives an asymmetrical plan to the whole.

In the centre, in addition to the pool already mentioned, is a large
building (*watilan*) used for cock-fights. It is remarkable for its beamwork comprising two independent parts each resting on two concentric rows of pillars. Although the technique used is different, the
external appearance of the structure is similar to the Javanese *pendopo* or open-sided pavilion, which usually has three levels of roofs
(some *watilan* also have three such levels). In this building one can
see how the transmission of Javanese models was only formal and the
Balinese adapted their own techniques to forms which were new to

them. The methods used by the builders of the mosque at Demak in Java, which seems similar, were in fact different. They adapted a form for a function which was not that of the *pendopo*, but kept both the form and the technique, which the master builders were able to adapt.

The other buildings at Mengwi are the *meru* (Fig. 33) or towers used for offerings, which are sometimes decorated with salacious reliefs illustrating the fables of the *Pancatantra*. The *meru* (one is shown in the reliefs at Candi Jago in East Java, dating from the thirteenth century) comprises a raised box-like altar containing a statue and topped by multiple-tiered roofs similar to the false storeys of Javanese temples, but much higher, and of course in different and perishable materials. Often the central part of the shrine is surrounded by a portico of pillars placed on a masonry foundation.

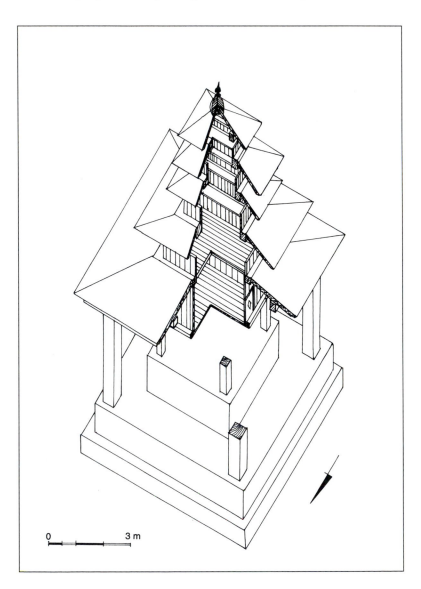

Fig. 33
The *meru* (B in Fig. 31) at the temple of Mengwi, Bali.

1. General view of the site of Dieng. (Jacques Dumarçay)

2. Candi Puntadeva at Dieng. (Jacques Dumarçay)

3. Borobudur, north side. (Jacques Dumarçay)

4. Borobudur, balustrades of the first and second galleries, north side. (Jacques Dumarçay)

5. Borobudur, the fourth terrace forming the base of the circular terraces. (Jacques Dumarçay)

6. Borobudur, relief on the lower level of the first gallery, on the west wing of the north side. (Jacques Dumarçay)

7. Ceremonial dining hall at the Sultan's palace in Yogyakarta. (Jacques Dumarçay)

8. Litter in the Sultan's palace in Yogyakarta. (Jacques Dumarçay)

9. Candi Kalasan, the first Buddhist temple in Java. (Jacques Dumarçay)

10. Candi Apit, a small shrine in the central enclosure at Prambanan. (Jacques Dumarçay)

11. Candi Sewu, an early Buddhist shrine in Prambanan; photograph taken before the restoration of the monument. (Jacques Dumarçay)

12. Close-up of Candi Sewu; photograph taken before the restoration of the monument. (Jacques Dumarçay)

13. Candi Plaosan, the vast Buddhist temple near Prambanan. (Jacques Dumarçay)

14. Side elevation of Candi Plaosan. (Jacques Dumarçay)

15. Candi Sambisari near Prambanan, after excavation. (Jacques Dumarçay)

17. South-west corner of Candi Singosari in East Java. (Jacques Dumarçay)

16. Candi Jawi, a temple showing Buddhist and Shivaite influences. (Jacques Dumarçay)

18. Goa Gajah in Bali. (Jacques Dumarçay)

19. Entrance to the main temple in Bangli, Bali. (Jacques Dumarçay)

20. Entrance to the inner enclosure of the temple of Mengwi, Bali. (Jacques Dumarçay)

22. The *meru* of Pura Danu, Bali. (Jacques Dumarçay)

21. The fountain representing the churning of the sea of milk in the temple of Mengwi, Bali. (Jacques Dumarçay)

23. A village in Lombok in the south-west of the island. (Jacques Dumarçay)

24. Houses and granaries in the village of Palawa in Sulawesi. (Jacques Dumarçay)

Ulu Watu

The positioning of the shrines plays an important part in their layout. This is particularly so in the case of the temple of Ulu Watu, built on a tiny western-facing peninsula jutting out into the ocean. The temple comprises an enclosure divided into two parts, the westernmost ending in a vertical drop some 200 metres into the ocean.

This temple is entirely built of coral stone obtained from a nearby quarry still in use (it is located some 250 metres north-east of the temple). When one arrives at the outer enclosure or courtyard, the *jaba*, at the top of the access stairway, there is a group of modern buildings to the south containing the images of Brahma, Vishnu, and Dwijendra, and to the west is the temple proper. Each part of the temple (the *jero* or middle courtyard and the *dalem* or inner courtyard) is entered after passing through monumental gateways completely different from those at Mengwi. The stone used allowed the carvers more freedom, resulting in split gates (*candi bentar*) ending in curved wings. The wall separating the middle from the inner court is broken by a corbelled arch (*candi kurung*) guarded by Ganesha figures.

The small temple of Tanah Lot owes its fame entirely to its extraordinary situation on a tiny peninsula just off the south-west coast.

Batur and Bratan

Lake Batur is located slightly off-centre of the island, and overlooking its shores is found a temple similar to that of Mengwi, but with the gateways built of black volcanic stone which gives a very austere appearance to its imposing edifices, dominated by the active volcano and lake. On the shores of another lake, Bratan, probably on the site of an old Buddhist shrine, is the Pura Danu (Plate 44). This is small, but remarkable for its site on a small isle in the lake; it only has two *meru*, one of which has eleven roofs raised one above the other (Colour Plate 22). This shrine is tended by the guild formed by people in charge of irrigation in the region.

Klungkung

The Kerta Gosa in Klungkung, a small town to the east near the foot of Gunung Agung, was the court of justice of the Rajah of Klungkung. The group of buildings is surrounded by an enclosure doubled on the inside with a moat going round a terrace. On this is built a rectangular-shaped open structure, the roof of which has radiating beamwork supported by carved king-posts in the shape of chimera. The fame of this building lies not in the beamwork, which unusually is concealed behind a ceiling, but in the decoration of the ceiling, with traditional paintings showing the sufferings of those who break the law. Within the enclosure but outside the moat is another building, square this time, with a painted ceiling illustrating a text relating the epic of life. These paintings are recent; the originals were painted in about 1840, but they were considerably

44. General view of Pura Danu, Bali.
(Jacques Dumarçay)

restored after a fire at the palace in April 1908. When the Dutch,
shortly after, built the court of justice they could not sit on the
ground, as the Balinese judges did, and the very curious armchairs
found in the pavilion were carved for them.

Temples of the North Coast
On the north coast, the temples have a noticeably different plan.
Pura Beji, for example, near Sangsit, encloses a flat terrain in which
is found a pyramid supporting the throne where the gods come to
sit. Although the scale is quite different, it recalls in some respects
the ancient Khmer temples, especially in the reduced heights given
to each level and the enhancement of the perspective of the staircase
by the reduction of its width as one climbs it. The monument is
built of abundantly carved brick showing a magnificent decor of
plant life into which stone carvings of faces sometimes appear.

The temples are only the shell for sumptuous rituals which are performed according to a very complicated calendar marking the days
deemed auspicious. There are two methods of measuring time:
Saku, which follows a calendar similar to the Gregorian one, and
Wuku, a year of 210 days divided into thirty weeks of seven days.
The priests interpret the different conjunctions of dates in one cycle
with the other, often adding other calculations, and making the
choice for the date of a ceremony splendidly complicated. The cre-
mations of the nobles are occasions of extraordinary festivals, and for
the least ceremony a procession of women bearing extremely elabor-

86

ate offerings is held. Nevertheless, what one sees today in the midst of the fervour of belief is only a survival: Balinese civilization suffered an immense setback when the Dutch attacked the palace of the Rajah of Badung in Denpasar in 1906. The rajah, seeing he could not win, held a *puputan* or mass suicide of himself and most of his family and supporters. Balinese artists continue to practise but from that fatal date their art has lost the royal context which gave it much of its original strength.

Denpasar

The modern city of Denpasar has few interesting monuments. However, the Museum Bali, on Jalan Major Wisnu, is a handsome architectural group built in 1925 on the initiative of the then director of archaeology, F. J. Kroom, by a German architect, Kurt Grundler. The museum has a rich collection of objects from the island, and several traditional buildings have recently been erected in the courtyard. Near Sanur, another museum was built in 1933 for the Belgian artist Le Meyeur; it has a heteroclite collection, sometimes amusing, located next to the sea.

Lombok

The island of Lombok is separated from Bali by the deep Lombok Strait. The first accounts of the island date from the tenth century. Like Bali, it is dominated by a high volcano, Mount Rinjani (3775 metres). The island was colonized by the Balinese from the seventeenth to the nineteenth centuries, but they appear to have remained a minority constituting the governing class. In 1885 there was a revolt by the indigenous inhabitants, the Sasaks, against the Balinese, who had forced them to take part in the internal wars then devastating Bali. The Sasaks sought the aid of the Dutch to free them of Balinese control. In 1894 the Dutch organized a conference between the two sides; the Balinese were constrained to pay a war indemnity and the Dutch remained in the capital, Mataram, until the indemnity was paid. The Balinese attacked the Dutch and were badly beaten, and the Sasaks participated in some degree to the defeat of their former conquerors. Finally, in 1895, Lombok was annexed to the Dutch East Indies, and the fate of the Sasaks hardly changed, Dutch rule being no more benevolent than Balinese. The Sasaks again revolted in the east in 1902 and the west in 1906; sporadic revolts continued until the establishment of Indonesian independence.

The cultural sites of Lombok are readily divided into two, the Balinese sites and the Sasak sites. The Balinese monuments are naturally mostly in the west of the island (with some exceptions, notably the village of Shela which is well to the east); Sasak sites cover most of the island. The Sasaks turned to Islam in part as a protest against the Hindu Balinese, in part under the impulsion of Javanese proselytizers, seemingly in the latter part of the sixteenth century.

The Hindu temples of Lombok are similar to those in Bali but seem to be constructed on a much larger scale. Most of them have suffered in frequent wars and have been rebuilt with little care, as with the Pura Samudra on the west coast. However, in villages (Colour Plate 23) one can see survivals of ancient Balinese techniques which have disappeared in Bali itself. The rice granaries (Fig. 34) are raised on piles and covered with thatch resting on a beamwork made of hoops; this is a very old Indian tradition which has almost entirely disappeared in the land of its origin. The shape is found in Cambodia, but the techniques used to produce it are different, and it is unknown in Java. The rice granaries of Lombok must be all that remains of the first wave of Indian influence in Bali (Plate 45).

The Muslim sites are better maintained and there are some fine mosques with exceptional architecture. This owes its origins to Java and goes back to structures which can be found in the reliefs at Candi Jago (dating from the end of the thirteenth century). The buildings have radiating beamwork supported by a single pillar; obviously the technique does not allow for a large space to be roofed

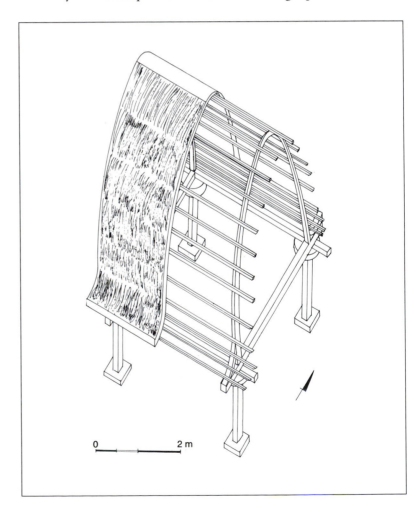

Fig. 34
A rice granary in the south-west of the island of Lombok.

0   2 m

88

45. A rice granary, built in the old Indian tradition, in Lombok. (Jacques Dumarçay)

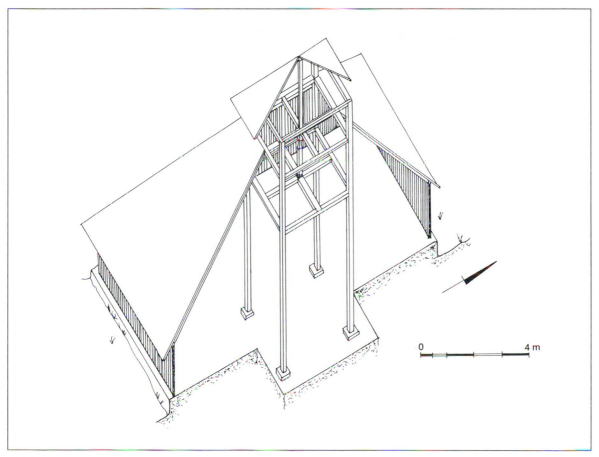

Fig. 35
The mosque of Pengadangan in Lombok.

over, so the Lombok builders completed the structure with an external wall supporting the rafters. Sometimes, under Balinese influence, the central pillar does not go down to the ground but rests on an intermediate beam, as in the *watilan* of Balinese shrines. Because these buildings are extremely fragile, they are frequently restored; those at Bayan and Semokan are traditionally replaced every eight years, and each renewal is the occasion of modern additions. In spite of that, certain buildings have kept their old form or at least it can easily be reconstituted. This is the case with the mosque at Pengadangan (Fig. 35), in the east of the central part of the island, where the beamwork can be seen in the prayer hall. The building has a square plan and a masonry base; in the centre are four pillars supporting two beam frames. Into these is inserted a crossing of beams supporting two king-posts, one above the other. This unusual technique leaves the room completely free in the centre, and the mihrab indicating the direction of Mecca is correctly oriented to the west. Externally, the walls are formed by vertical planks, and the roof is thatched. The entrance door has two panels, and the windows are closed by a single shutter which opens inwards. In its extreme simplicity, this architecture is a fitting expression of the calm life of the Sasaks on Lombok.

6　Sulawesi and the Moluccas

Sulawesi

THE Kingdom of Gowa was located in the south of Sulawesi, also known as the Celebes (Fig. 36), which played an important role in the region in the sixteenth and seventeenth centuries through its important fleet of galleys. The administrative capital, Makassar, now Ujung Pandang, was a centre for the spice trade, even though its soil was not suitable for the cultivation of spices, serving as a focal point between Ambon, Banda, and the smallest of the Molucca Islands which were given over almost entirely to the cultivation of nutmeg and clove trees, sought after by Chinese, Indian, Arab, and European merchants. The nutmeg tree supplies two spices; the nutmeg proper, and mace, which is the dried aril of this nut, formed between the nut and the shell. The floral buds and fruit-bearing stalks of the clove tree provide cloves.

After the seizure of Malacca by the Portuguese, in 1511, Malay and Achinese merchants removed to Makassar. The King of Makassar at the beginning of the seventeenth century, after conquering the Toraja lands, allowed the Dutch to set up a trading office. But the Dutch, being already dominant in Ambon, did not tolerate competition, and began the conquest of Makassar in 1661, which was not completely subdued until 1669.

Ujung Pandang (Makassar)

The town of Makassar before the Dutch conquest was described by the French missionary Nicolas Gervaise, whose work was first published in 1688. He spoke of, *inter alia*:

its situation a little above the mouth of a river ... built in a very fertile plain, abounding in rice, fruit, flowers, and all kinds of vegetables. The walls of the town are lapped on one side by the waters of this great river.... Only the palace of the king and some mosques are built of stone, all the other dwellings are of wood, but they are nonetheless most agreeable, for the wood is of different colours; ebony ever predominates, and all are worked with so much art, and the pieces so well inserted in each other, that it seems that the whole house is only made of a single block of wood in different colours. The biggest of these buildings does not exceed four or five *toises* [some 8 to 10 metres] long, by one or two wide; the windows are very narrow, and are almost all covered by very large thick leaves, which rain does not penetrate.

91

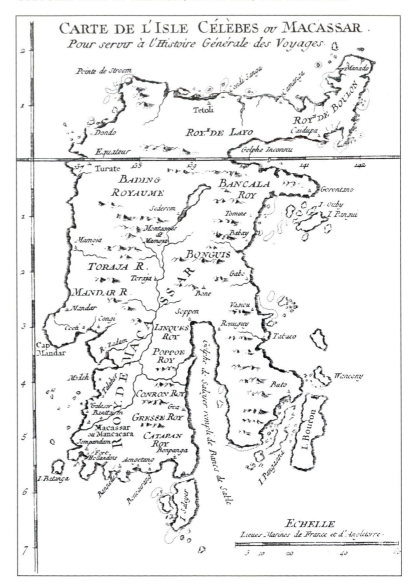

Fig. 36
Map of the Celebes (Makassar), from the *Histoire générale des Voyages* of Abbé Prévost, published between 1746 and 1769.

The Dutch chose another harbour for their boats, affording rather better shelter, in the the Bay of Bonthain (Fig. 37).

The Dutch partially destroyed the fortifications of Sultan Alauddin built in 1634 and on the site of the Gowanese fort began to build a fortress, following the Treaty of Bungaye in 1667, known as Fort Rotterdam. This, rebaptized Benteng Pannyua, occupies a very large area close to the sea-shore, and has been converted into a museum and cultural centre; its collection of Chinese ceramics on display is of considerable interest. These were mostly found locally, and were extensively used as grave objects in the animist pre-Islamic period; as the dead had to be honoured so that they would not return to torment the living, they were buried with as much wealth

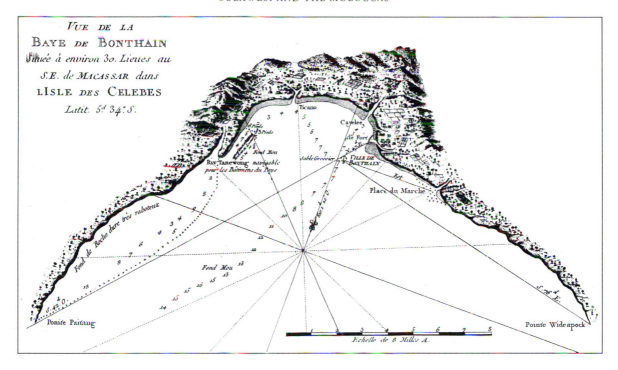

Fig. 37
Map of the Bay of Bonthain, from the atlas of Nicolas de Fer, published in numerous editions from the 1750s.

as the living could afford. The rich clothes which also accompanied the bodies to the world beyond have, of course, all disintegrated.

The Javanese hero Prince Diponegoro (1785–1855), who led the revolt against the Dutch from 1825 to 1830, was, after his capture, first of all deported to Menado in the north of Sulawesi, and then to Makassar, where he spent more than twenty years incarcerated in Fort Rotterdam until his death. His tomb is located in a small cemetery naturally located on Jalan Diponegoro.

A little outside Ujung Pandang is the large wooden palace of the Sultans of Gowa at Sunggaminasa; this is a typical structure of the nobility in the eastern part of the Indonesian archipelago.

Tanah Toraja

The Toraja people were not converted to Islam, and live in the centre and the south of Sulawesi. The name derives from a Bugis word *toriaja* meaning 'men of the mountains'. The Bugis from Makassar traded Indian cloth, Chinese porcelain, and Dutch and other coins in return for slaves and, later, coffee. Though now nominally Christian, the animistic beliefs of the Toraja involved an extremely elaborate ancestor cult, which gave rise to very curious tombs, of which some good examples can be found in the cliff at Lemo (14 in Fig. 38). Places for the coffins were cut into the cliff face, sometimes as much as 20 metres above the ground, which meant that their insertion was a very complicated operation, as the coffins were extremely heavy. When the burial ceremony is completed, which includes the sacrifice of several buffaloes, pigs, and chickens, wooden

93

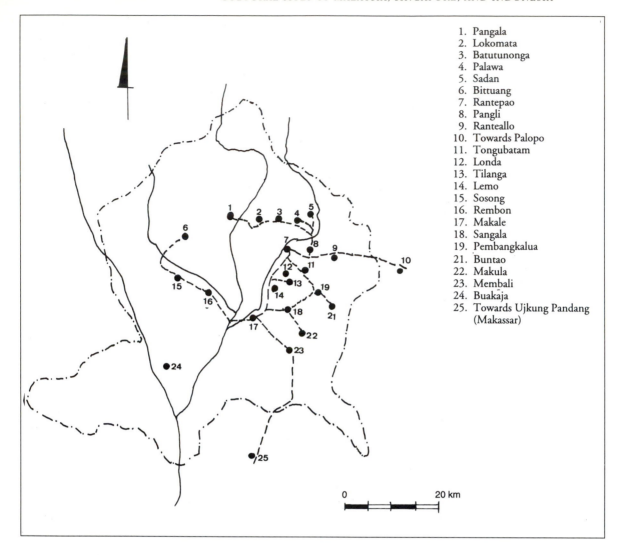

1. Pangala
2. Lokomata
3. Batutunonga
4. Palawa
5. Sadan
6. Bittuang
7. Rantepao
8. Pangli
9. Ranteallo
10. Towards Palopo
11. Tongubatam
12. Londa
13. Tilanga
14. Lemo
15. Sosong
16. Rembon
17. Makale
18. Sangala
19. Pembangkalua
21. Buntao
22. Makula
23. Membali
24. Buakaja
25. Towards Ujkung Pandang
    (Makassar)

Fig. 38
Main sites in Tanah Toraja, Sulawesi.

effigies of the deceased wearing the clothes of the recently departed appear to gaze down and watch over the living from a high balcony.

The traditional houses, known as *tongkonau*, of Toraja villages, which formerly, before rice cultivation was introduced, occupied the tops of the hills rather than the valleys, are enormous structures with huge saddle-backed roofs, and are faced by smaller rice barns in the same form. Both have decorated and coloured gables, usually sporting a buffalo head. No nails are traditionally used, and the roofing was originally overlapping strips of bamboo, but alas, is now most often rusting corrugated iron.

The shape of these houses goes back to the time of those represented on the early bronze drums of the Dong Son period, though the original techniques have disappeared. The characteristic roofs (Colour Plate 24; Plates 46 and 47), good examples of which can be seen at Palawa, Marante, and Nanggala, outside the small township

94

46. Toraja houses with their distinctive saddle-backed roofs in the village of Palawa in Sulawesi. (Jacques Dumarçay)

47. Close-up of the roof of a Toraja house. (Jacques Dumarçay)

CULTURAL SITES OF MALAYSIA, SINGAPORE, AND INDONESIA

of Rantepao, derive from an ancient method of beamwork construction combined with the desire to obtain a large internal area; this was based on the tension of the ridge beam. After it became impossible to continue this technique, because of the disappearance of sufficiently large boles in the forests, the builders used an ordinary beamwork, the projections of which are supported at each end on pillars; this considerably reduced the internal volume but keeps the external appearance of the structure.

The magnificence of these structures, notwithstanding their present roof covering, the majestic scenery which surrounds them, and the extraordinarily elaborate funeral rites of the Toraja make their region one of the most distinctive in Indonesia.

The Moluccas

The trade in spices, particularly in cloves and nutmegs, found its origin in the Moluccas (Fig. 39), a group of islands to the east of Sulawesi and the west of New Guinea, where these trees grew naturally. In the sixth century, nutmeg was already being traded in Aden, but one of the earliest descriptions of the tree and its fruit was given by the Chinese Chai Ju-kua in the thirteenth century:

The tree resembles the Chinese juniper and attains a height of upwards of an hundred feet. Its trunk and branches, with foliage, present the appearance of a large shady roof under which forty or fifty men may find protection. When the blossoms open in the spring they are taken off and dried in the sun.... The fruit resembles the nut; when the shell is removed the pulp can be kept a long time, if preserved in ashes ... its properties are warming.

Many subsequent descriptions appeared.

There were three different routes for the spice trade to reach Europe. Before Vasco da Gama, the spices were transported first from the Moluccas to Malacca, then from there to Calicut on the Malabar coast of India. The shipment then left for Aden and the Red Sea, and was carried overland to Suez and Alexandria, where it was shipped again to Venice, which had almost complete control of the trade in Europe. Vasco da Gama, in 1498, rounded the Cape of Good Hope on a route prepared by the work and patronage of the Portuguese prince, Henry the Navigator (1394–1460); at first only the Portuguese used this route, soon everyone did. In 1869, the opening of the Suez Canal to the passage of boats transformed the route to the Indies, reducing the distance by one-third.

After the Portuguese had conquered Malacca, they occupied the Moluccas at the early part of the sixteenth century, but even before Malacca was lost to the Dutch in 1641, they had been replaced by the Dutch, who had already penetrated the area from the beginning of the seventeenth century. The Dutch were determined to obtain a monopoly of the spice trade, and to avoid the nutmeg germinating elsewhere, they lightly grilled all the nuts before exporting them. This effort to obtain a monopoly also involved uprooting trees on

96

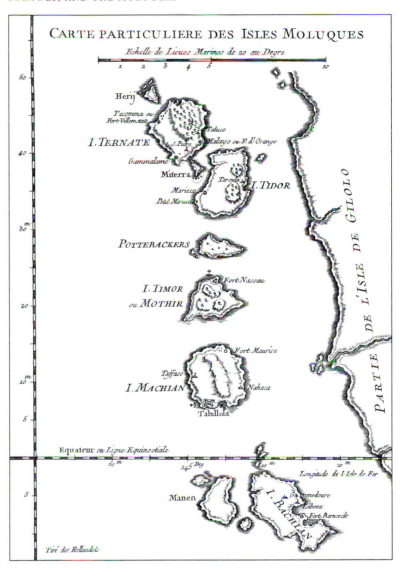

Fig. 39
Map of the Molucca Islands, from the
Histoire générale des Voyages of Abbé
Prévost, published between 1746 and
1769.

certain islands where they grew naturally, to concentrate production
in particular areas, and led to tragic events like the extermination or
enslavement of the Banda islanders, and the massacre of the English
in Ambon in 1623. The VOC was wound up in 1798, with massive
debts, and the Moluccas were occupied by the British on two occasions during the Napoleonic wars, after which the return of the
Dutch was the occasion of more blood-letting. The Moluccas also
had a troubled history during and after the Second World War.

Ternate and Tidor

These were the most famous of the clove islands. The Portuguese
arrived in Tidor in 1511, and ten years later, the remains of
Magellan's fleet, the *Victoria*, commanded by del Cano, landed
there. The Spanish bought a cargo of spices which was transported

back to Spain; it was even given out that Magellan's attempt to circumnavigate the world had no other aim but to acquire spices.

The inhabitants of these islands had converted to Islam shortly before the arrival of the Portuguese, and some had taken refuge in the mountains, refusing conversion. In this uncertain situation, the Sultan of Tidor asked the Portuguese to build a fort. They refused, and instead built a fort at Gamalama on Ternate. When the Dutch occupied the island after 1608, they set up their centre at Talangame, where the Portuguese had previously set up their clove stores. The bay of Talangame was suitable for the anchoring of vessels but the modern town of Ternate is a little to the east of this.

On Ternate, the sultan's palace, a mansion-like building now a museum, can be visited, along with four ruined forts: Orange (Oranje), a vast Dutch enclosure; Kayuh, once occupied by the English; by the beach, Kastella, now disfigured by a road passing through it; and Toloko, which is perhaps in the best condition of the lot. The remains of a Portuguese chapel dedicated to Our Lady also survive.

Ambon

The history and natural wealth of the island of Ambon, to the south of Tidor and Ternate, are known thanks to the work of two extraordinary men, the naturalist Georg Rumphius (1628–99) and François Valentijn, a Protestant clergyman with an interest in geography and history. Rumphius, who became blind in 1670, spent much of his life in Ambon working for the Dutch East Indies Company, and Valentijn spent two long periods there, from 1686 to 1694, and 1705 to 1713; his historical and descriptive work covers not only the Dutch possessions but much of what was known of Asia at the end of the seventeenth century.

The town of Ambon is located at the edge of a very deep bay which makes for a well-sheltered harbour. The Portuguese period in Ambon left its mark chiefly in religion; St Francis Xavier worked as a missionary in Ambon and elsewhere in the Moluccas in 1546 and 1547, and Ambon remains staunchly Catholic, in spite of the Dutch presence and a degree of assimilation, as well as superior pastors like Valentijn. On a more secular note, the Portuguese influence is seen in the romantic ballads known as *keroncong* accompanied by a Portuguese guitar.

In about 1650, the Dutch declared a monopoly of the island's spices, working through the authority of village chiefs. The Ambonese, in contrast to many other groups, were treated with consideration by the Dutch and their loyalty was rewarded; after the fall of Malacca, Makassar, and, in 1682, Banten to Dutch rule, the monopoly was effective, though some Ambonese took local boats, known as *kora-kora* (Fig. 40), filled with spices, which they offered to foreign merchants at lower prices.

Nothing remains of the Portuguese fort in Ambon, known only through early engravings which show stonework bound by mud and

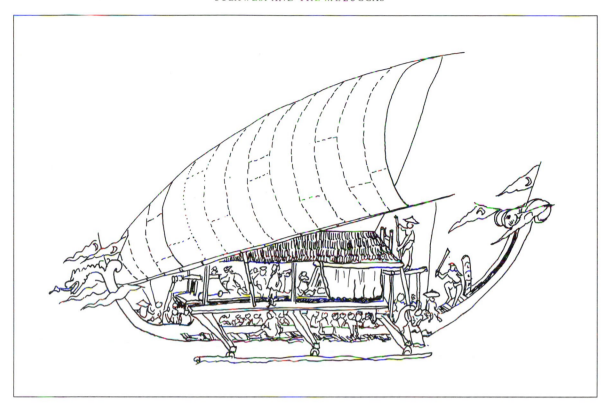

Fig. 40
Kora-kora, from the *Atlas* of the VOC, published *c.*1750.

wood. The Dutch improved the town, constructing a fort at the edge of the bay, and canals. Their fort, Nieuw Victoria, was completed in 1775 and still remains, its porch framed by a classical architectural motif of four Roman Doric pilasters upholding a pediment. This is not the only fort on the island; the VOC built others at Larike (Fort Rotterdam), Lima (Fort Haarlem), and also on the shores opposite Ambon at Howamohel, Haroehoe, and Saparoea. At the end of the eighteenth century, this group of fortresses made Ambon virtually impregnable.

The Banda Islands

The small group of seven islands collectively known as Banda lies south-east of Ambon. The Portuguese first arrived in 1512, the Dutch in 1599, the English (on Run Island) in 1601, and the Spanish in 1606. It was here that the nutmeg and mace were most assiduously produced. The Dutch Governor-General Coen, in 1619, took decisive steps to control the Bandas and, in 1621, with a fleet of thirteen ships attacked Lonthor, the largest and most important island, almost completely wiping out the local population, and replacing it with slaves and Javanese convicts. A class emerged of Dutch-licensed planters known as *perkenier* which grew very wealthy. The remains of their villas can be seen in the chief town, Bandaneira, on Neira Island. The ruins of Fort Nassau, originally

99

Fig. 41
Boat appearing in the carvings at
Borobudur, south side, second gallery.

20 cm

0

built by the Portuguese, are at the back of the town, and above it is the much larger Fort Belgica, a pentagon with towers at the angles, started by the Dutch in 1611. The most important fort militarily, Fort Hollandia, was built on Lonthor after Coen's attack on the island, but it was virtually wrecked in an earthquake in 1743.

Dependence on a single crop inevitably brought about its own decline. When the British occupied the islands during the Napoleonic wars, nutmeg seedlings were taken to Penang, Ceylon, and elsewhere, and successfully planted. The Dutch monopoly was broken, and the introduction of refrigeration reduced the necessity of spices to preserve meat, leaving them as exotic garnishings for the wealthy.

Fig. 42
Boat appearing in the carvings at
Borobudur, north side,
first gallery.

20 cm

0

Movement between all the islands in the region was effected on
boats whose shapes has remained virtually unchanged since the
eighth century. There is considerable similarity between the *kora-kora* of the eighteenth century and the boats which appear on the
carved friezes of Borobudur (Figs. 41 and 42). Continuity thus pre-
vails within the region and over time.

7 Conclusion

IN South-East Asia, as everywhere else, the transition of a site from village to town was accomplished in innumerable stages and this is also true of the decline of any site. Most of those considered in this book and our preceding volume, *Cultural Sites of Burma, Thailand, and Cambodia*, did not have a complete evolution; either their function became specialized, for example, the Dieng plateau in Java or the island of Muara Jambi in Sumatra, where, for a time, the occupation was exclusively religious, or the site was abandoned because of external pressure, as with the collapse of the Joho dam above the town of Plered.

In spite of the extreme diversity of the sites where the civilizations of South-East Asia reached material form, not to mention the differences of religion, political organization, and sociological evolution, it is still possible to extract some common ground.

The formation of urban agglomerations in the region was only marked from the ninth and tenth centuries, when the authority of local rulers was sufficiently assured to undertake such an enterprise. Town plans were not drawn up for large populations, but for the expression and protection of the governing authority (this is not particular to South-East Asia: the town of Richelieu, constructed on the orders of the cardinal close to his chateau, only contained 2,000 inhabitants). Even when the plans cover a large area (Angkor Thom or Majapahit, for example), each is laid out with the pedestrian in mind. The horses, elephants, chariots, and wagons frequently found on reliefs probably did not occupy a very important place in intra-mural circulation. To cross Angkor Thom on foot takes a little under an hour; this is also the case with old Banten. The care taken with the visual aspect of the town's monuments, mostly from the point of view of a standing spectator who looks straight ahead at the architecture, is another example of the manner in which the city was conceived. There are very few monuments constructed for which the spectator's oblique viewpoint was necessary; the pentagonal temples at Pagan, the central tower of Angkor Wat, the upper terraces of Borobudur or Candi Jabung are exceptions to the dominant frontality.

Beyond its practical destination as a seat of power, the town also carried another image, another expression of authority, found in its divine origin. This is most obvious at Angkor Thom, the city of the Khmer King Jayavarman VII, but can also be seen at Singosari in East Java. These towns reflect an imaginary reality which is appreciated as each is unravelled. The inhabitants, when moving about these cities, gave them the fabulous dimensions separating the elements found there of Mount Meru, and the chains of mountains and oceans which surrounded it.

However, the cultural sites of South-East Asia, as several scholars (notably Denis Lombard and Anthony Reid) have noted, changed in both form and function. During the fifteenth century, there was a shift from an agricultural to a mercantile society, the main aim of which was the commercialization of spices.

Commerce was always important for South-East Asian civilizations. It was probably the transactions with Tang China that allowed for the development of Srivijaya in the eight and ninth centuries. But what caused the commercial take-off of spices, in about 1400, was the increasing demand for them under the Song dynasty in China and in Europe after the Crusades.

This change in mentality, though profound, only superficially transformed the nature of the sites. Spices are agricultural products which require care in their cultivation. Admiral de Beaulieu, when he passed through Aceh in 1621, after a detailed description of pepper cultivation, concluded, 'from what has been said, it can be seen that pepper is not found like sand on the seashore'. The care of clove trees requires hard weeding and trimming operations, and the harvesting and drying of cloves are undertakings demanding care and skill. For such cultivation, a large peasant population was needed, which had to be fed; when the requirements of rice cultivation were overlooked in the choice of a site, the consequence was not long in making itself felt, as was the case with Aceh.

The sites in the region only developed in the framework of strong authority. When in the tenth century, perhaps because of the destruction of embankment works on the Opak River, the weakened rulers abandoned Prambanan, the village authorities acted independently but no new site really emerged. This is also true of Cambodia; there, during the reign of Jayavarman VII a considerable change was effected in the method of irrigating the site; the great reservoirs were abandoned and dam-bridges, scattered all over the kingdom, were substituted, giving local authorities a say in the matter of water distribution, which they did not have before; they found they were gradually ever more independent of the central government but incapable of undertaking any great enterprise.

When, after a break, construction works were undertaken again, they were not on the scale of those at Pagan, Angkor, or Prambanan, and gradually led to the disappearance of architectural artifices, which gave another vision to architecture in relation to a fixed viewpoint, and, in consequence, to a rigid form of urbanization. On the other hand, the symbolic charge borne by structures increased considerably: the palaces of the sultans of Solo and Yogyakarta, whose architectural qualities are distinctly modest, are veritable symbolic pictorial puzzles which have to be deciphered; this is also true of Mandalay, Bangkok, and Phnom Penh.

Today the silhouette of Angkor Wat appears on the Cambodian flag and Borobudur has become the palladium of the Indonesian Republic; modern states are thus linked to a prestigious past. Most of the sites have been arranged so that a large number of visitors can be accommodated: this is not without some ambiguity, for many if not most were conceived for the select few. The changes which time has brought to the sites have considerably altered the architectural approach and the surrounding space. The monuments of Pagan rise in a now arid landscape; in Angkor, the forest has invaded everything; in Thailand, the monuments of Phimai and Lopburi are plumb in the middle of modern towns, and in Java, Borobudur, Plaosan, and several others, the sites are surrounded by cultivated fields.

Restorers have also had varied viewpoints, sometimes even in regard to the same structure. At Angkor, the restorers at first stressed the early thirteenth century (partially or completely eliminating everything posterior to this), which gave splendid coherence to a particular site, but as new discoveries were made, the site lost this unity in favour of a clearer historic vision. A similar attitude is probably shown in Borobudur, where a corner of the added base has been uncovered to show the first state of the base of the monument, but the early arrangement of the hill and the great access stairways have not been restored, which is to be regretted.

The visitor to the cultural sites of South-East Asia thus has to make a very great effort of imagination to reconstitute the monuments in their ancient context which is not always self-evident. The intrusive forest of Angkor gives a particular charm to the architecture but disturbs its meaning. The temples of Dieng, all their architectural context having disappeared, today seem lost in the middle of a volcanic crater with no direct relation to the site, of which they were nevertheless an integral part.

The architectural themes and the layout of the ancient sites of South-East Asia are so far removed from us today that their emotive appeal has become foreign to us. The modern visitor brings his own culture and recomposes these sites. This phenomenon is not recent and was always in the minds of the master masons who feared their buildings would be misunderstood or even rejected; to avoid this, they introduced into the buildings elements which were easily understood by everyone. Thus Borobudur was built in stone in an area where constructions in wood dominated, but so that the visitor would not be too bewildered by the new material, the master mason caused butt-ends to be carved in the stone, suggesting a wooden floor. This signal referred to a context known to everyone, and inserted the novelty of Borobudur in the architectural framework of the time, helping in its interpretation. These signals are no longer understood by the visitor nor are they even readily discerned, as wooden buildings have almost entirely disappeared, and when they do comprise part of a spectator's personal references, entirely different techniques are involved.

The falling into ruin and any subsequent restoration furthermore adds a new approach to the buildings; this is particularly true of Prambanan. The surrounding wall of the innermost enclosure of the monument has been partially destroyed, which allows for an overview of the central structures and sight of their perspective effects which are only coherent from certain points inside the enclosure, and cannot be properly appreciated beyond the entrance pavilions to it. Still at Prambanan, the 224 dependent shrines in the second enclosure have for the most part been destroyed, and this partial ruin eliminates a screen designed to exist between the main temples and the visitor entering the site. Furthermore, the ruin of dependent shrines has also transformed the concept one has of other adjacent sites, notably Candi Sewu and Candi Plaosan. When the religious transformations are partial, as, for example, the shift from Vishnuism to Buddhism at Angkor Wat, the visitor undertakes for himself a mixture of the elements he sees, or sometimes gives disproportionate importance to more recent additions; an example would be the French writer Pierre Loti, who visited the monument in 1901, and whose dominant impression of Angkor Wat was the gallery known as the Gallery of the Thousand Buddhas.

To see is often to recognize; so that many visitors to Bruges conjure up the image Venice. This is true in South-East Asia where, in front of Candi Shiva at Prambanan, one recalls the central sanctuary of Angkor Wat, and at Borobudur, the Mingalazedi at Pagan, one's memory seizing on a particular element and causing all the differences between the two to be overlooked. In most cases the overall composition of the sites (Angkor Thom is an exception) has been lost, and one has to recompose this, often from elements of subsequent periods. This recomposition depends on the individual, and becomes a personal creation from one's own experience. There is nothing to regret in this: visiting and reinterpreting the architecture and the urban composition of sites gives a new breath of life to places which otherwise would be dead cities.

The major sites of the region impress all, as they were intended, though perhaps not in the same manner in which they were intended (how many visitors to Borobudur follow through the story of the birth, life, death, and transmogrifications of the Buddha as depicted in the sculptures of the galleries?). The minor sites have their individual charm and they give their contribution to the overall cultural history of the region as well. It is hoped that this book, and its preceding volume, will have given the modern cultural pilgrim sufficient background and food for thought on the greatness of past civilizations which find their continuities in the nation-states of today.

Glossary

balai	a roofed hall with pillars and open sides
baray	a large man-made water reservoir in Cambodia
cella	the enclosed body of a temple
dalem	the inner courtyard of a Balinese temple
jaba	the outer courtyard of a Balinese temple
jero	the middle courtyard of a Balinese temple
kulkul	a hollowed-out tree-trunk used for sounding the alarm at a Balinese temple
meru	a tower used for offerings at a Balinese temple
mihrab	a niche in a mosque used to show the direction of Mecca
Pancatantra	a collection of Indian fables
pendopo	an open-sided pavilion
vajra	a symbol of the lightning of the god Indra
watilan	a building used for cock-fights

Select Bibliography

Abdullah bin Abdul Kadir (1969), *The Hikayat Abdullah,* translated by A. H. Hill, Singapore: Oxford University Press.

Bernet-Kempers, A. J. (1991), *Monumental Bali,* Berkeley/Singapore: Periplus.

Bosch, F. D. K. (1961), *Selected Studies in Indonesian Archaeology,* The Hague: Martinus Nijhoff.

Brown, C. C. (trans.) (1976), *Sejarah Melayu or Malay Annals,* Kuala Lumpur: Oxford University Press.

Casparis, J. G. de (1956), *Selected Inscriptions from the 7th to the 9th Century AD* (Prasasti II), Bandung: Masa Baru.

Covarrubias, Miguel (1937), *Island of Bali;* reprinted Kuala Lumpur: Oxford University Press, 1972.

Crawfurd, John (1828), *Journal of an Embassy to the Courts of Siam and Cochin China;* reprinted Singapore: Oxford University Press, 1967.

Dumarçay, Jacques (1986), *The Temples of Java,* translated and edited by Michael Smithies, Singapore: Oxford University Press.

_____ (1991a), *Borobudur,* translated and edited by Michael Smithies, 2nd edn., Singapore: Oxford University Press.

_____ (1991b), *The Palaces of South-East Asia: Architecture and Customs,* translated and edited by Michael Smithies, Singapore: Oxford University Press.

_____ (1993), *Histoire de l'Architecture de Java,* Paris: EFEO.

Graaf, H. J. de (1977), *De Geschiedenis van Ambon en de Zuid Molukken,* Franeker: Wever.

Guillot, Claude (1990), *The Sultanate of Banten,* Jakarta: Gramedia.

_____ (1994), *Banten avant l'Islam, Etude archéologique de Banten Guirang (Java, Indonésie), 1932–1526,* Paris: EFEO.

Jacq-Hergoualc'h, Michel (1992), *La civilisation de ports-entrepôts du sud Kedah (Malaysia) Ve-XIVe siècle,* Paris: L'Harmattan.

Loeb, E. M. (1935), *Sumatra: Its History and People;* reprinted Kuala Lumpur: Oxford University Press, 1972.

Lombard, Denys (1967), *Le Sultanat d'Atjeh au temps d'Iskandar Muda, 1607–1636,* Paris: EFEO.

_____ (1990), *Le carrefour javanais, essai d'histoire globale,* Paris: Ecole des Hautes Etudes en Sciences Sociales.

Marsden, William (1811), *The History of Sumatra;* reprinted Kuala Lumpur: Oxford University Press, 1966, and Singapore: Oxford University Press, 1986.

Miksic, John (1985), *Archaeological Research on the 'Forbidden Hill' of Singapore: Excavations at Fort Canning, 1984,* Singapore: National Museum.

——— (1989), 'Urbanization and Social Change: The Case of Sumatra', *Archipel*, 37: 3–29.

Pigeaud, T. (1960–63), *Java in the Fourteenth Century*, Vols. 1–V, The Hague: Martinus Nijhoff.

Pires, Tomé (1944), *The Suma Oriental of Tomé Pires*, edited by A. Cortesão, 2 vols., London: Hakluyt Society.

Ramseyer, Urs (1977), *The Art and Culture of Bali*, Oxford: Oxford University Press.

Ricklefs, M. C. (1974), *Jogyakarta under Sultan Mangkubumi, 1749–1792*, London: Oxford University Press.

Smithies, Michael (1981), *A History of Modern Indonesia*, London: Macmillan Press.

——— (1986), *Yogyakarta: Cultural Heart of Indonesia*, Singapore: Oxford University Press.

Stutterheim, T. (1956), *Studies in Indonesian Archaeology*, The Hague: Martinus Nijhoff.

Vandier, Pierre (1714), *New Atlas*, Leiden.

Vlekke, B. M. H. (1960), *Nusantara, a History of Indonesia*, The Hague: W. van Hoeve.

Wheatley, Paul (1960), *The Golden Khersonese*, Kuala Lumpur: University of Malaya Press.

——— (1964), *Impressions of the Malay Peninsula in Ancient Times*, Singapore: Eastern Universities Press.

Wolter, O. W. (1975), *The Fall of Srivijaya in Malay History*, Kuala Lumpur: Oxford University Press.

Index

Numbers in italics refer to Colour Plates.

Location of the
Main Sites Mentioned
in the Text